PENGU

Fierce Bad Rabbits

'Pollard so delicately enters into the world of "sweet treats, acrobats and laughter," that the reader feels they are rediscovering once-loved landscapes' *New Statesman*

'Most people's primal cultural memory is that of being read to by a parent. This is a phenomenon most sensitively and intelligently explored in *Fierce Bad Rabbits*' *Daily Telegraph*

'There's memoir as well as cultural history here, and monsters and magic aplenty as it strays into the very darkest corners of fairytale forests' *Guardian*

'Excellent' *Daily Mail*

'It will make you think again about why you loved children's stories, and it will lead you to new discoveries too. A happy reconnection to the serious joys of childhood' *Harper's Bazaar*

'The combination of scholarly research and witty writing makes for a thoroughly enjoyable book' *Spectator*

'A wonderful read' *Choice*

'A celebration of picture books and their artists to spark your own childhood memories' *Evening Standard*

ABOUT THE AUTHOR

Clare Pollard is an award-winning poet and playwright based in London. She is the author of five poetry collections and the editor of the *Modern Poetry in Translation* magazine. She is striving to build the perfect picture-book library for her two small children.

Fierce Bad Rabbits

The Tales Behind Children's Picture Books

CLARE POLLARD

PENGUIN BOOKS

PENGUIN BOOKS

UK | USA | Canada | Ireland | Australia
India | New Zealand | South Africa

Penguin Books is part of the Penguin Random House group of companies
whose addresses can be found at global.penguinrandomhouse.com.

First published by Fig Tree 2019
Published in Penguin Books 2020

001

Copyright © Clare Pollard, 2019

The moral right of the author has been asserted

Text from *Flower Fairies of the Spring* by Cicely Mary Barker
courtesy of Frederick Warne & Co. Ltd., 1923.
Text from *Flower Fairies of the Wayside* by Cicely Mary Barker
courtesy of Frederick Warne & Co. Ltd., 1948.
Eric Carle, 'The Art of Fiction no. 299' from *The Paris Review*. Copyright © 2015,
the Paris Review, used by permission of The Wylie Agency (UK) Limited.
Text from *The Tale of Mrs. Tiggy-Winkle* by Beatrix Potter courtesy of
Frederick Warne & Co. Ltd.
Text from the 2016 Philippa Pearce Lecture 'John Wayne and Sibelius
or The Train Has Rain in It' courtesy of Allan Ahlberg.

Typeset by Jouve (UK), Milton Keynes
Printed and bound in Great Britain by Clays Ltd, Elcograf S.p.A.

A CIP catalogue record for this book is available from the British Library

ISBN: 978-0-241-35479-7

www.greenpenguin.co.uk

For Cate

This is the sort of book we like
(For you and I are very small),
With pictures stuck in anyhow,
And hardly any words at all.

You will not understand a word
Of all the words, including mine;
Never you trouble; you can see,
And all directness is divine –

Stand up and keep your childishness:
Read all the pedants' screeds and strictures;
But don't believe in anything
That can't be told in coloured pictures.

Inscribed by G. K. Chesterton to
a young friend, in a picture book
by Randolph Caldecott

Contents

List of Illustrations

Introduction

Opening a picture book from your childhood can be dangerous.

To relive those bedtime stories so exactly, image by bright image, is to feel overwhelmed by how much else is irrecoverable: that room, your small body in pyjamas, your bear propped on the pillow, a parent's voice.

For me, the book I must be most careful of is Hilda Boswell's *Treasury of Poetry*. A few years ago my mother found my old copy, and brought it to London with her when she visited from the North. On the forest-green cover a boy and girl look towards a town with a castle and a bridge over a silver river. A rainbow frames them like a door. There are also, if you look carefully, by the roots of the trees and in the clover, tiny supernatural creatures with blossom bonnets and black eyes. The boy has bare feet; the girl wears a pink slip. They will walk down the hill into a new world.

Inside the cover it says:

TO: CLARE,
FROM: AUNTIE SUSIE AND UNCLE ARTHUR
XMAS 1980

I was two. I have no recollection whatsoever of an Auntie Susie or Uncle Arthur. Perhaps they were my fairy godparents.

That day, I opened the book and looked at the introduction Hilda Boswell wrote in 1968 for the first edition. 'I have made this book especially for you,' she said. 'But not just for you, also for myself; not the present, grown-up self but the old self, the one left behind in childhood.' And the book was a doorway for me too – I stepped through the rainbow and was small again.

One illustration shows images of cats and elves in a fire's flames. 'I like to sit at the fire and stare / At the curious things I can see in there' – a poem by the grand-sounding Irene and Aubrey de Sélincourt. Had I ever looked at a fire and not heard those words? Another poem, 'A Summer Morning' by Rose Fyleman, tells of a little girl impelled to run towards the woods, 'so far, so fast'. It is only on her arrival that she understands what brought her there: 'On every leaf of every tree / A fairy sat and smiled at me!' And beside it Boswell's picture of pale fairies in the tremulous glade. How many summer mornings I had scanned the trees for them. How I had longed for that vision, like William Blake's vision of angels!

With every page, my stomach lurched with some lost intensity. There was July, bringing 'apricots and gilly-flowers'. There was Charles Kingsley's 'The Lost Doll', her 'arms trodden off by the cows, dears' – yet still beautiful to her owner. There was the spider luring me into his parlour.

Graham Greene wrote, in his essay 'The Lost Childhood', that 'in childhood all books are books of divination', and that 'like the fortune teller who sees a long journey in the cards or death by water they influence the future'. This treasury, I realized, was the book that made me a poet. But more than that, I could see how it shaped my feelings. The pages were full of kindness: a bird bought to set it free; a coat to keep a little frog warm. And every page glowed with the wonder of being in the world: 'The poppy's in the corn; / I'm glad that I was born.'

In no time at all, I was crying. I told myself it was the hormones. That, and the question of whether it is better to be born or not is the kind of thing that gets pregnant women going.

In truth, pregnancy made me anxious. I had never been anxious and I was uncomfortable with this new self. I was becoming more like my mother. I love my mum very much but I didn't want to *be* her, especially not circa 1982, always working herself into a stew with worry about us. We used to tease her about being 'sacrificial', the way she gave us the choicest bits of food at dinnertime, and I knew that she had given up her own ambitions as a writer when she started a family. Since falling pregnant I fretted about that glass of wine, my age, the odds on the Down's test, my lack of maternity pay (I was self-employed). In bed at night, I agonized over the right position for the baby's blood supply; twisted uncomfortably. I stopped eating what I wanted and ate what I was supposed to. I stopped thinking about my literary hopes, because they were over. That was it. With a baby, how would I write a great novel or break into movies or edit a magazine? It was impossible. I would never find the time, and anyway I was too old now.

I have always looked forward. In my poetry collections, I never dwelt on my childhood. I rarely thought about it even, especially since my dad died of cancer at fifty-three. It seemed such a bitter-sweet self-indulgence. I must confess, I never even allowed myself to miss people, or not in the way other people seemed to talk about it. I loved my dad more than anyone in the world, but I didn't exactly miss him. Or, that is, I never thought: *I wish my father was here to see this,* or *I'd like to talk to my father now.* I didn't let myself think like that.

But my life was over. I was becoming a mother, and, as a friend said over coffee: 'It's not about you any more, it has to be all about the children.' I was moving to the edges of my own existence. This brought with it, along with the cravings for sweet-and-sour sauce and whole tubs of yoghurt, a disorientating nostalgia. I started to remember the time when I was a small child myself: everything still lying possible before me.

I found myself online ordering picture books. *The Bears' Picnic. Burglar Bill. Bread and Jam for Frances.* It was bad luck to order them. I hadn't even bought any tiny vests yet, and the baby would need those far sooner. But the baby was just an excuse, I was ordering them for myself. For, in Hilda Boswell's words, 'not the present, grown-up self but the old self, the one left behind in childhood.'

*

My childhood was ordinary in the best sense. Picture-book ordinary. I was brought up in a village outside Bolton called Edgworth. It had woods and reservoirs and verges full of meadowsweet, and three churches and five pubs. There was a store, Jack Holden's, that sold the most wonderful ice cream made of condensed milk that people would travel miles for, an off-licence, a newsagent, a butcher's shop, a greengrocer, a pharmacist, a gift shop and a chippy (where a red sausage always sat in its moist glass coffin). My grandparents ran the Post Office on the hill, and on the day I was born my father, half-crazed with excitement, yelled up to their window: 'Wake up, it's a little girl!'

My mum mainly looked after me and my little sister, but she also ran a playgroup in the cricket club with a friend, where her hand-puppet, Mrs Crow, told the story at circle time. My dad was deputy head of the village primary school, so every morning he would put on his suit and set off down the street to cries of 'Morning, sir!' A travelling library would come to the village occasionally: a caravan full of books, which seemed to me as thrilling as the circus coming to town.

I never had much sense of rich or poor before I was a teenager, though both must have existed – everyone just had their job: milkman, lollipop lady, landlord, nurse. In 1981 the average mortgage rate hit 17 per cent. My parents had overstretched themselves to buy our bungalow and, looking back, I realize this caused my mother a lot of stress. We would wear hand-me-downs and get second-hand Sindy dolls for birthdays; there were arguments over whether we could afford branded biscuits. But as a child I barely noticed. All the children went to the same school and their years were marked by the same milestones: Lent, school disco, paddling pools, harvest festival, bonfire, fairs, carols, sponsored run. Bedtime was after *Coronation Street*. Occasions were marked by pop and crisps or the epitome of Northern mass-catering: a meat and potato pie served with pickled beetroot and red cabbage.

Once I saw, I was certain, a flower fairy in the undergrowth. Sometimes, my father would take us to the woods and we would play Pooh-sticks in the river by the waterfall. Or we would go for a walk, with sandwiches, joking that my mum was like Papa Bear in Jan and Stan Berenstain's *The Bears' Picnic*, always looking for somewhere better to sit. 'When is this spot-picking going to stop?' Once, because I loved Russell and Lillian Hoban's book *Best Friends for Frances*, I stole the idea of holding a girls-only picnic, and one girl's shoe got stuck in the mud by the reservoir.

The place I grew up and the books I read there can be hard to separate out.

What stories do we tell our children?

Looking at these books decades later, with adult eyes, I began to wonder. Picture books had shaped my own childhood. I would read them over and over to my children, until we all had them by heart. Until they in their turn would be, as Graham Greene so beautifully puts it, going to their bookshelves, 'taking down the future and opening the pages'. Before I passed these stories on, shouldn't I interrogate them a bit more thoroughly? Where was the serious analysis of *Burglar Bill*? Google many preschool classics that have sold millions, and you will only find reviews at the level of 'an appealing story (Ages 3–6)' or 'this zany delight will have children in fits of laughter' or 'wonderfully thick, durable pages', but I believe that these stories are more than diversions, they are teaching our children how they should be.

Picture books have become a great leveller. Whatever your class, everyone recognizes a picture of Paddington or Peter Rabbit or the Gruffalo. Picture books are one of the few areas of culture we still have left that is shared by all. Political leaders are even pressured to show they are in touch with ordinary people by citing their favourites. (Interestingly, this simple PR exercise often goes wrong. George Bush named Eric Carle's *The Very Hungry Caterpillar* as his favourite childhood book although, to many observers' delight, it wasn't published until he was twenty-three, while David Cameron had the nerve to name Dr Seuss's anti-capitalist fable *The Lorax* and then misremember its plot.) Since the publication of *Babies Need Books* (1980) by the New Zealand bookseller Dorothy Butler, everyone also seems to agree that picture books are a common good, helping not only communication skills and literacy but parent–child bonding by giving a shared 'frame of reference'. In the UK books are considered so essential for development that the government gifts them to every child via their Bookstart programme, where they are handed out by health visitors in England and Wales at the same time they check your baby's pincer grip. Studies suggest the number of books in a young child's home is a major indicator of later academic achievement.

Not all books though, surely, are of equal merit. There is an enormous gulf between the ones that seem cut-and-pasted by committee (stock photos of babies clapping or pulling faces supposedly denoting 'sad' or 'happy', 'textural' soft and bumpy bits, heavy use of flaps, the urgent need to find some animal or other) and the ones that aspire to art. Bruno Bettelheim, a child psychologist, wrote in his influential book about fairy tales, *The Uses of Enchantment* (1976), that children need books that make life 'meaningful to them'. He was deeply frustrated with picture books and reading primers 'designed to teach the necessary skills, irrespective of meaning' – vacuous stories that did not stimulate the deeper imagination. I would argue that some of the great picture books of the last century do indeed manage to enrich life. Memorized by millions at that crucial age when their sense of self is developing, picture books can very easily be used to indoctrinate us into the unthinking acceptance of hierarchies and behaviours. But through them, children can also be afforded a glimpse of life beyond their own tiny world; a glimpse of other futures, of other sorts of happiness or hope.

When my son was born I began collecting picture books more seriously, building a dream library – a library to open up his thousand possible lives. I would ask my mum to rifle through stalls at fairs and jumble sales; scour the shelves of Oxfam; go in Sense every time I pushed the pram down Peckham High Street, looking for the bashed-up spines and wonkily Sellotaped pop-ups of much-loved favourites, diverting my literary ambitions into parenting. By the time Gruff was one we were on ten books with his cup of milk every night:

Dear Zoo
Where's Spot?
That's Not My Monster
Monkey and Me
Peepo!
That's Not My Car
Fox's Socks
Maisy Goes to the Cinema
Brown Bear, Brown Bear, What Do You See?
Hairy Maclary from Donaldson's Dairy

And I began thinking about them too – learning about the cultural history of the picture book, from its beginnings in the 1800s with Edward Lear and *Struwwelpeter*, through Babar and *Goodnight Moon*; then the golden era of Maurice Sendak, Shirley Hughes, Eric Carle and Judith Kerr. It was fun to analyse them as I might a poem; to share facts with other weary parents – how *We're Going on a Bear Hunt* was based on a folksong, and *Green Eggs and Ham* uses only fifty words. I began to notice rhyme schemes and neologisms; to theorize about the ubiquity of sausages and bunnies. At first it was a way to keep my brain busy during those toddler afternoons when time is turgid, made up of endless renditions of *row-row-row your boat* or peekaboo tedium. Slowly, I realized I was writing a book again. Motherhood wasn't incompatible with writing after all; my children were teaching me new ways to look and read and speak about the world.

And then those sudden seconds – your child lifts a flap and hisses like a snake for the first time. They point proudly at a blue horse.

1. The Butterfly's Ball

On adult authority

Where do my memories begin?

It shocks me, the number of people who say they recall nothing before school. I feel more like Beatrix Potter, who was laughed at for saying she could 'remember quite plainly from one and two years old'. To me, one of the best passages of prose ever written is the opening chapter of Laurie Lee's *Cider with Rosie* (1959). It exactly captures the state of being a toddler with 'antennae of eyes and nose and grubbing fingers'. He describes those towering grasses 'tattooed with tiger-skins of sunlight'; family faces 'of rose, familiar, living'; water that breaks and shines on the tiled floor. I too recall an abundance of those slow strange days, their muddled clarity: dusty chickens on a path; briar-rose petals stirred to brown to make perfume; the smell of home-made play-dough; powdering my sister's bum; the hosepipe's pattering rainbows; a foxglove the colour of fever I could never touch.

But do I really remember? My father was such a teller of stories. What is really mine, and what is instead a vivid imagining of a much-repeated tale? Stories are powerful things. Plato said that 'those who tell stories rule society'. When we are small, the stories adults tell us shape our world, our selves, our memories.

The stories they choose to tell about our childhood, in a way, become our childhood.

Our bungalow, on a new estate called Moorfield, was, I realize now, contrived by my dad to look like a pub, probably in order to piss off his strict father who was part of the Temperance movement. It had wooden panelled walls, horse brasses, leather furniture, a soda siphon, ashtrays, a dart board, a low hush of smoke in the air. The football pools were always waiting near the door for collection. We had a Turkish-patterned carpet in faded peacock colours. He would paint the ceiling by standing on the glass coffee table and stippling the plaster until it looked like royal icing, and once his foot crashed through. My dad was useless at DIY – my mother hung the wallpaper – although legend has it he did once knock out our old bathroom with Uncle John while I sat in the cot, a preternaturally calm baby, turning over the pages of my Ladybird books for hours.

It is also difficult to say for certain when picture books begin. The term 'picture book' is now usually used when pictures and text are of equal importance, with an illustration on every page or pair of facing pages, and the book is aimed at children who cannot read or are just beginning. They are distinct from, say, graphic novels (like Hergé's *Tintin* series) or illustrated novels (such as Roald Dahl's, with those glorious, scrappy Quentin Blake illustrations).

There have been claims that the first picture book is

the *Orbis sensualium pictus*, published in Nuremberg in 1658. It was created by a tragic teacher and priest from Bohemia called Jan Komenský, who had lost all his belongings in a fire and all his family to the plague. For much of the Thirty Years War, a wanderer exiled from his homeland, he was witness to the suffering of child refugees, who he decided he wanted to help. The *Orbis sensualium pictus* disseminated his unusual educational technique of teaching the alphabet via animal noises (you make the sound *r* as the dog 'grinneth', *w* as the hare 'squealeth', *l* as the wolf 'howleth') with a woodcut illustration beside each letter. Such was its lasting impact that it was treasured a hundred years later by a young Goethe.

Afterwards, there were many other illustrated tomes aimed at children, but like Komenský's they tended to be educational tools: ABCs or moral lessons. John Newbery's *A Little Pretty Pocket-Book* (1744) offered improving fables and a list of 'One Hundred and Sixty three Rules for the Behaviour of Children' which must have been a real bedtime favourite. (Sample rules: 'Approach near thy Parents at no Time without a Bow', 'Dip not thy Meat in the Sauce', 'Spit not in the Room, but in the Corner, and rub it with thy Foot, or rather go out and do it abroad.')

For those adults who despair of the tiaras and weapons now stuck to the cover of every magazine, it's worth noting that even in 1744 the (gender-specific) free gift was being pioneered as an inducement to reading – *A Little Pretty Pocket-Book* was originally sold with a ball for a boy and a pincushion for a girl, both half-red and half-black. A pin was stuck in the red side to mark a good deed, and the black to mark a bad one, in order to 'infallibly make Tommy a good boy, and Polly a good girl'.

These books are clearly on the side of the grown-ups. They are teaching tools with designs on shaping and disciplining. The picture book as we might recognize it – as a fully illustrated tale – had yet to appear.

Perhaps our story really begins with this memorable invitation:

> Come take up your Hats, and away let us haste
> To the *Butterfly's* Ball, and the *Grasshopper's* Feast.
> The Trumpeter, *Gad-fly*, has summon'd the Crew,
> And the Revels are now only waiting for you.

Whoever is speaking, their voice has the ring of authority. With everyone waiting, it is difficult not to fold to the social pressure and reach for our hat.

These are the first lines of *The Butterfly's Ball, and the Grasshopper's Feast*, which was composed by an adult of considerable real-world authority, the MP William Roscoe, in 1802. It was initially illustrated by William Mulready. I first read the poem in Hilda Boswell's *Treasury of Poetry* with her own dreamy illustrations – the androgynous moth with its parted lips; the spread of rosehips and tiny lily-pads; fairies nibbling crumbs under the table – and remember loving the sound of Roscoe's fancy words, although I didn't know their meaning: *viands, repast, minuet.*

Written by Roscoe for his ten children as a celebratory *jeu d'esprit* to memorialize the birth of his youngest son,

Robert, the poem was first published in *The Gentleman's Magazine*. Its popularity led to it being republished as a stand-alone book, which was one of the first to have colour illustrations. Some editions had hand-coloured images, probably completed by young children working on an assembly line in sweatshop conditions (the gap between the sentiment attached to the idea of a child and care for *actual* children is, I should warn you, often stark in this history).

The book, notably, aims to entertain rather than elucidate. Some of Roscoe's contemporaries struggled with this, searching frantically for a moral – the Irish author Mary Leadbeater wrote in a letter in 1811, 'I apprehend Roscoe's Butterfly's Ball must have been written to remove the dread and disgust of insects so prone to fasten upon a youthful mind, and if it could prevent this evil early in life it must be allowed to be a meritorious performance.' The text, however, clearly doesn't do anything of the sort. It is a glorious party, with sweet treats, acrobats and laughter – a party enjoyed not by human adults, but by 'the children of earth and the tenants of air', the homeless, the dirty, the young, the tiny, the squashed and stamped upon, and 'you' – dear reader – on whom they all wait.

It would be neat to see *The Butterfly's Ball, and the Grasshopper's Feast* as a poem that defeats the forces of authority, the primers and sermons, and ushers in the anarchic new age of the picture book. Certainly Edward Lear, who we will soon see unleashing nonsense upon the world of children's literature, seems to have enjoyed it in his youth. But the truth, of course, is more complex – it is always the adult who writes children's books, illustrates them, publishes them, buys them. Adult desires (to educate the child, to keep it quiet, to make it sleep, etc.) did not just disappear.

Jacqueline Rose famously claimed that 'children's fiction is impossible' because the 'child' that children's fiction is aimed at is always an adult construct (*The Butterfly's Ball, and the Grasshopper's Feast* was not, for example, aimed at the actual child labourers colouring its pictures). Even the name 'children's fiction' is a sleight of hand that erases adult involvement. With picture books there is a whole extra layer of adult interference, as the preliterate toddler cannot experience the story without a parent or carer mediating it for them (and often, as I do, changing vocabulary, skipping, unpacking, emphasizing, doing the voices, pointing things out). Children's fiction, such as it is, Rose suggests, usually relies on creating a 'child' within the text, and then inducing the young audience to identify with it, as Roscoe did when he inserted his little son Robert into his verses.

The trick is to persuade both the grown-up reader and the child who listens that you are on their side.

The Butterfly's Ball, and the Grasshopper's Feast did this so successfully it became a phenomenon, spawning hundreds of imitations with names like *The Peacock 'At Home'*, *The Lion's Masquerade* and *The Fishes' Grand Gala*. (Roscoe himself also produced *The Butterfly's Funeral*, but surprisingly that wasn't such a hit.)

The poem creates a sense of carnival, of the world

turned upside down, but we should remember that carnivals are usually state sanctioned. They release pressure in a manner that protects the status quo. *The Butterfly's Ball, and the Grasshopper's Feast* was much loved by the royal family. Rebellion is kept within the party, within the pages, and anyway sticks close to civilized behaviour. In this case insects mimic the hierarchies of humanity, attending formal 'balls', laying aside their stings, setting the table neatly, reminding us – as the occasion ends – that at such a late hour we should 'hasten home'.

My early pleasure in poetry was bound up with nonsense. 'Be alert,' my dad would counsel. 'The world needs more lerts.' When I woke up in the middle of the night as a baby, my dad always lulled me back to sleep by rocking me to 'I Am the Walrus' by the Beatles. Our family had many invented words. 'To squink' (*verb*), for example. If we were all sharing a can of pop on a day trip and you sipped it, you had to be aware of the binding rule that you then had to carry it: 'The one who drinks it squinks it.' My mum and I played rhyming games for hours, generating gibberish. When I was two I took to calling the local marmalade cat a 'jam ham'.

Another of my favourite pages in the *Treasury of Poetry* is Edward Lear's description of the delightfully random cargo the green-headed Jumblies pick up, having ignored everyone's advice and gone to sea in a sieve:

> And they bought an Owl, and a useful Cart,
> And a pound of Rice, and a Cranberry Tart,

And a hive of silvery Bees.
And they bought a Pig, and some green Jack-daws,
And a lovely Monkey with lollipop paws,
And forty bottles of Ring-Bo-Ree,
And no end of Stilton Cheese.

'Ring-Bo-Ree' made me thirst as 'forty bottles of apple juice' never could have done. It was a thirst for the world of pure imagination; for the impossible. Even then, I was a good 'Polly'. Perhaps I also thirsted for the Jumblies' defiance.

Edward Lear's *A Book of Nonsense* (1846) is, in the history of English picture books, the next great leap, and one further still away from the didactic tradition. If books were meant to drill sense into children, this explicitly did its opposite. Edward Lear was a fascinating character – the twentieth of twenty-one children, neglected by his mother and afflicted by terrible epilepsy which always made him feel an unmarriageable outsider (in his diary he recorded his fits with an X). He was, despite this, very successful. As well as being one of the great ornithological illustrators, producing birds for both of John Gould's famous books of birds and *The Zoology of the Voyage of H.M.S. Beagle*, he was also a drawing master for Queen Victoria, and a friend and sometime member of the Pre-Raphaelites.

The constant tension between insider- and outsider-dom, authority and anarchy, finds its way into his *Book of Nonsense*, which he began both writing and illustrating at Knowsley Hall. Engaged there by Edward Stanley, the

18

13th Earl of Derby, to sketch the estate and draw plates of the 'Knowsley Menagerie', Lear began concocting rhymes to entertain the earl's grandchildren. He was sometimes welcomed into the earl's family, at other times sharply aware he wasn't one of them. It was the period of the Corn Laws, soldiers firing on Chartists, a general unease. Knowsley was a home for the establishment, but the company could also be surreal: reptiles, zebras, a platypus and a bandicoot. (It was later turned into Knowsley Safari Park – a monkey stealing your windscreen wipers becoming a memorable event in many Northern childhoods.)

A Book of Nonsense is mainly comprised of limericks – five-line rhyming poems with an AABBA structure and roughly anapaestic metre. As a folk-form, limericks are often linked to transgression and the violation of taboos, which perhaps appealed to Lear's subversive side. In these limericks there is often a struggle against an oppressive 'they'. 'They' tell the Old Person of Hurst he'll get fat; smash the Old Man with a gong for making too much noise; smash the Old Man of Whitehaven for dancing a quadrille with a crow, etc. (there is a lot of smashing). 'They' seem to be those in power; the crowd; the system. Lear's sympathies with the individual pitted against societal prejudice make the limericks feel very contemporary.

However, Lear's verses are also just extremely random: sometimes tenderly daft, sometimes wincingly dark (a woman bakes her husband in an oven; a man shuts his wife in a box and says 'Without doubt / You will pass all your life in that box'). The giddy pictures that accompany each of them are what make the book such a work of genius – they don't just illustrate but interact with the limericks: elaborating, shifting the tone. It is this which has led some to claim *A Book of Nonsense* as the first true picture book. We read, for example, that:

> There was an Old Man with a nose,
> Who said, 'If you choose to suppose,
> That my nose is too long,
> You are certainly wrong!'
> That remarkable Man with a nose.

Take the limerick on its own, and it is easy to sympathize with this Old Man who refuses to conform to society's physical ideals. In the accompanying image, though, we can see his nose, more like an elephant's trunk, is actually forcing screaming people to leap out of its way.

On a first read, the final lines of Lear's limericks can feel disappointing. The rhythm – with those two shorter, more urgent lines – and the anticipation created by the rhyme scheme lead us to expect a punchline. But Lear never delivers one, only repeating the first line with subtle tweaks. Nothing changes. The Old Man still has a long nose. The antithesis of teacherly, these poems explicitly refuse to go on a journey or teach a moral lesson.

In the last lines Lear sneaks in some of his own, invented adjectives ('ombliferous', 'umbrageous') as if to leave us even more at a loss.

*

At the same time as Lear was putting together his *Book of Nonsense*, just before Christmas in 1844, Dr Heinrich Hoffmann went into Frankfurt to look for a book for his three-year-old son Carl. It was a time of festive markets, brimming with candies, nuts and toys. Candles shivered in the cold. Hoffmann, a medical man who worked at a mental asylum, found nothing but moralizing tales that began with assertions such as 'children must keep clean', so instead he bought a blank exercise book, and told his wife, 'We are going to make a book of it.' After Christmas he circulated it amongst friends. Zacharias Löwenthal came across a copy and urged Hoffmann to let him publish it. On a 'bright wine-influenced whim' Hoffmann consented, although he used the pseudonym Reimerich Kinderlieb (meaning 'the rhymester who loves children').

Der Struwwelpeter himself, with his eyrie of hair and meat-hook nails, was a character Hoffmann often drew for his younger patients to distract them from anxiety and pain. His intention was not to terrify children, but to laugh with them at the underlying savagery of existing didactic texts that revelled in the nasty consequences of misbehaviour. But as Marina Warner has written, it is in fact 'a good example of an author's intentions failing to control the impact of his work, for it still is, for all its happy ironies, a nasty book.' Ever since, while some of his three- to six-year-old readers have been amused by these 'funny stories and droll pictures' (as the original title had it), a great many more have found them bed-wettingly terrifying.

Hoffmann brought together two common juvenile plot lines, both popularized by his Danish contemporary Hans Christian Andersen. The first presents us with a pure, innocent child who is called early to their Lord's side in heaven. Early children's books are full of such death scenes, with the best example still read today perhaps being Andersen's 'The Little Match-Girl', snowflakes caught in pretty curls, dreaming of her grandmother in the flare of her last moments. The second portrays the bad child who is punished – as in Andersen's ferocious tale 'The Red Shoes' where Karen is brutally punished by angels for her vanity, her feet unable to stop dancing even after she has them amputated.

Both these narrative arcs are parodied by *Der Struwwelpeter*, in which misbehaviour leads swiftly to a brutal, meaningless end. A boy declares he will no longer eat soup and dies five days later, lighter than a sugarplum; lighter than a thread. A boy goes out in a storm and is blown away, never to be seen again. Little Suck-a-Thumb, most famously, sucks his thumb and – alack – the scissor-man flies into his house with enormous scissors and 'Snip! Snap! Snip!' removes his thumbs, the stumps of which bleed copiously on to the floor and into nightmares.

Having come to *Der Struwwelpeter* as a grown-up, it's the story of Harriet, who plays with matches and is burnt to death, that I find most disturbing. Her Mamma and Nurse have left her alone. She finds the flames 'pretty'

and is ecstatic with joy when one burns 'so clear'. Only
her pets witness her death:

> The Pussy-cats saw this
> And said: 'Oh, naughty, naughty Miss!'
> And stretched their claws,
> And raised their paws:
> ''Tis very, very wrong, you know,
> Me-ow, me-o, me-ow, me-o,
> You will be burnt, if you do so.'

Like a Greek chorus, their warning cannot stop the
inevitable tragedy. Harriet's apron strings catch fire and
we witness her fully aflame as if in self-immolation. 'Her
apron burns, her arms, her hair—/ She burns all over

everywhere.' The cats' tears make a pond. Only her scarlet shoes are left amongst the ashes, like proof of her wickedness (it is hard to believe this story doesn't allude to Andersen's match-girl and red shoes, although they are contemporaneous, both published in 1845).

To a modern reader, used to the concept of 'responsible adults', placing the guilt for a little girl's excruciating death solely on her own actions is hard to take. The cats' hiss of 'naughty Miss' and 'we told her so' exposes an ugly adult world that smears the innocent with its own carelessness.

This was also Hoffmann's point, surely, but it's not an easy point for a three-year-old to absorb. *Der Struwwelpeter* went on to inspire adult political humour (such as the 1941 *Struwwelhitler*), Hilaire Belloc's *Cautionary Tales for Children* ('Henry King: Who chewed bits of String, and was early cut off in Dreadful Agonies'), Edward Gorey's *Gashlycrumb Tinies* with its alphabet of infant deaths ('X is for Xerxes devoured by mice'). In picture book terms, though, it is hard to think of anyone who has since aimed such disturbing material at such a young readership. The mixture of authority and anarchy in Hoffmann's adult voice (and the parent's voice, as they read aloud to their child) is disturbing because it is so hard to interpret, especially across the centuries. It is like the voice of a sociopath who keeps everyone on their nerves, not knowing when to laugh or tremble. By the end a child is left barely able to distinguish bad from good; prank from horror. They do not know whether Hoffmann is on the grown-up's side or their own.

Still, perhaps that wasn't the case for Heinrich Hoffmann's little son Carl, who recognized his father's dark jokes, and who lived in a nineteenth-century Germany where every second child died. *Every second child!* To be a father or a son in that period was to live every moment with mortality in mind. Death in your mouth or in the weather.

Marina Warner has talked of these stories teaching laughter as a kind of 'strategic refuge' from the world's arbitrary suffering. Their function, she says, is to 'line the stomach'.

Carl Hoffmann died at age twenty-seven in Peru of yellow fever.

Being pregnant in the twenty-first century can sometimes feel like existing within a cautionary tale. The responsibility for children's suffering now lies, it is widely agreed, entirely with the mother.

'Sinead King: Who changed her cat's Litter Tray, and had a Miscarriage in Dreadful agonies'

'Ramona: Who absent-mindedly nibbled some Brie, and was rushed to an Emergency C-section'

'Kelly Horne: Who drank Prosecco at a wedding before she knew she was Pregnant, and had a Baby with Smaller than average Head Dimensions'

Being pregnant is also a reminder of how strange it is to be growing. To wake up every morning with your body somehow different: bigger, stranger, fuller. Little children live with this strangeness every day: you can fit through a door, then you can't. Your chair is too small. Suddenly, you can reach the secret cupboard.

Lewis Carroll's *Alice's Adventures in Wonderland* (1865) and *Through the Looking-Glass* (1871) are novels, not picture books, but they have had such an influence on the artists in our story that they are relevant – thousands of picture books are foreshadowed in the human-sized white rabbit hurrying past in his waistcoat, from Beatrix Potter's clothed bunnies to the rangy Mr Rabbit in Charlotte Zolotow and Maurice Sendak's *Mr Rabbit and the Lovely Present*. How to begin assessing the influence of the Drink Me potion's flavour of 'cherry-tart, custard, pine-apple, roast turkey, toffy, and hot buttered toast', or the innovative interplay of text and words that has the Mouse's tale a wriggling tail on the page, the gnat speaking in a tiny little voice?

There are also, importantly, the radical shifts in size and perspective: Alice falling down a rabbit hole, the tiny golden key, her body opening up 'like a telescope', swimming in a pool of tears, talking with a caterpillar. Shrinking and growing. Illustrator John Tenniel's picture of a giant Alice jammed in a room – head pressing against the ceiling, arm out of the window – is uncannily like a repeated bad dream I had as a teenager, where I found myself stuck and stooped in a house like a Wendy house.

It's always about power, of course, big and small: wanting and not wanting power; disappearing or becoming unignorable. Picture books are obsessed with scale – look at the miniaturism of *The Butterfly's Ball, and the Grasshopper's Feast* – and Alice's lurches between large and small lead to *Little Miss Tiny* in her mouse hole, *The Giant Jam Sandwich*, Dr Seuss's Who-ville (on a speck of dust on a clover flower), Jez Alborough's *Where's My Teddy?*, Julia Donaldson and Axel Scheffler's *The Smartest Giant in Town*.

Lewis Carroll is another nonsense writer with a fascinating life, caught between a hallucinatory, subversive dream-world and his reality as a buttoned-up Victorian. Carroll was born Charles Dodgson in 1832. Originally expected to join the church, he ended up a mathematician at Christ Church, Oxford, at the heart of the establishment. He had a stammer and referred to himself as the dodo (Do-Do-Dodgson), hence the dodo in Alice. He never married.

The contrast between his fantastical imagination and his repressed outer life has led to speculation – particularly as Carroll enjoyed the company of young girls and had an interest in photography, taking photos of them in costume or, occasionally, naked. There is a photograph of his muse, Alice Liddell, aged seven and uncomfortably self-aware, dressed as 'The Beggar Maid' with her tattered dress exposing a shoulder, chest, thigh; another of him kissing her, fingers grasping her waist. There is one of her elder sister, Lorina Liddell, nude and full-frontal. Although we may appreciate that Victorian culture is utterly alien to our own, with the age of consent being thirteen when the Alice books were written, it is hard not to be discomforted by a letter that says: 'one hardly sees why the lovely forms of girls should *ever* be covered up.'

Carroll clearly saw allies in children – others who had

to behave, to abide by the rules, to be seen and not heard, but who were clear-sighted about the absurdity of adults. If, as Jacqueline Rose suggests, all children's fiction is a kind of 'soliciting, a chase, even a seduction' of the child reader, this is something Carroll excelled at. In his books, at least, they embraced Carroll's anarchy as he ridiculed hierarchies and rituals (royalty, the tea party, the croquet game, the court room, school), and mocked characters like the Duchess, so fond of finding morals in things.

The essayist G. K. Chesterton's brilliant 'A Defence of Nonsense' (1902) asserts that true nonsense resists analysis, claiming proudly that no age but his own could have realized Lear's Quangle Wangle 'meant absolutely nothing'. Making sense is, in a sense, a trap, even as we're seduced into it. When Alice asks Humpty Dumpty to explain 'Jabberwocky' (in which Carroll famously invented the words galumphing and chortle), he declares airily that toves are 'something like badgers, something like lizards and something like corkscrews' and that a rath is 'a sort of green pig'. He is clearly making it up, trying to sound knowledgeable. Pontificating pompously; as are we, if we start asserting that we have decoded the poem. (I wonder, is this whole book me performing as Humpty Dumpty – pontificating self-aggrandizingly about silliness?) But nonsense also reveals the structures of language – particularly, in Lear and Carroll, of the language of reason and authority – and so can be satirical even as it flaunts its meaninglessness.

Not that such satire bothers the powerful, when it's so easy to dismiss as gobbledegook. The best way to neutralize criticism is to purchase it, so they (literally) patronized these writers and let them amuse the children. During his lifetime a rumour even developed that 'Edward Lear' was a pseudonym, and the true author was Lear's patron, the Earl of Derby – both men were named Edward, after all, and 'Lear' is an anagram of Earl.

The rich and influential eat the honey; wrap their money in money. They dance on by the light of the moon.

I remember my father, too, as an insider and outsider. He taught begrudgingly for the educational authorities, but was actually more interested in being liked by the village children. Once the head of his school made him dress as the Mad Hatter for a fair. The costume suited him well; anarchy and authority in tension.

Usually my father wore cheap suits, which hung well on his slim frame. A tie, a handkerchief folded in his pocket. He had a thick, untameable mess of dark hair, and amused blue eyes. Every morning after his shave, tiny scraps of bloodied toilet paper clung to the nicks on his chin. My dad always seemed to be heading out to lead assemblies, football, the PTA; dashing and relaxed in his role, chewing a stick of Wrigley's gum in his handsome mouth.

Although he was the deputy head, his whole self rebelled against society's idea of how a teacher should behave. He was a local 'character', always up for a party, a pint, a provocation, a bet on the horses, a competitive game of almost anything (chess, darts, tennis, holidays). So ludic, his favourite book was actually *Games People Play*. His anecdotes were tales of youthful mischief – punching a bully, breaking into a train shed; illicit fireworks and purple hearts.

The children of the village would often talk of the mythical uplands of Junior Two, in which Mr Pollard let you play rounders every day, practise mind-reading and do quizzes instead of maths. He taught flight by climbing on a table, then leaping from one desk to another. At playtime, he 'taxed' children's crisps, and one end-of-term he came back with a bin bag full of different-flavoured packets – chicken to Worcester sauce – that students had Sellotaped over every inch of the classroom as a thank you. They knew he loved the end of term as much as they did.

When Gruff was born and I became a mother, I too felt suddenly torn between responsibility and rebellion. It was my job to wipe and change and burp this tiny creature; to produce milk at appropriate intervals; to report to the various social workers and clinics in a timely fashion; to never leave the baby unattended for a moment. It was impossible, such ceaseless attentiveness, like being at sea in a sieve. Where once I had been utterly independent, society now expected me to politely ask for help at staircases; politely smile when random strangers told me I had dressed him inappropriately for the weather; politely listen while employers told me a new mother would add too much risk to a freelance job; politely sing along with the 'Wheels on the Bus' at library rhyme time. When they got to *the mothers on the bus go chatter-chatter-chatter*, it made me want to break something.

I wanted to be free but I kept biting my tongue. It occurred to me that this is what adulthood is. When my son had a screaming tantrum, I partially admired him.

By the mid-nineteenth century imaginative advances in children's books were being matched by technical advances. The McLoughlin Brothers were becoming the biggest children's publisher in America by adapting the old idea of hornbooks – text pasted or carved on to wood, bone or leather to stop it tearing, or even, in some parts of Europe, baked into gingerbread and then gilded. McLoughlin Bros., Inc. started mass-producing ABCs and counting books mounted on linen, so that children could play with them roughly. Around the same time London publishers Dean & Son began printing what were commonly known as 'toy books', often with mechanical features – the name itself suggesting education was not their priority. Dean & Son eventually moved into 'rag books' too, advertising them as 'quite indestructible' (their logo showed a Jack Russell in a tug of war with a bulldog). These were the precursors to the cloth books I was given when Gruff was born, often with clips to attach them to the pram – books to gum and paw at.

Colour was also transformed in this period – instead of the pictures having to be hand-coloured, chromolithography was used (a chemical process based on water rejecting grease). When Routledge and Warne contracted printer Edmund Evans, famous for his yellow-backs or 'Penny Dreadfuls', to produce toy books in 1865 the market galloped on at dizzying speed – first print runs soon exceeded 10,000. Evans himself became involved in choosing and commissioning artists including Walter Crane, Randolph Caldecott and Kate Greenaway, who were soon his best-known illustrators – often referred to as the 'Triumvirate'. Their experiments in relating text and image developed the picture book further, although many of their publications were still poetry anthologies, Birthday Books or songbooks rather than single tales. Reading them now, one also suspects they were often devised to titillate adult palates rather than amuse children – Caldecott's *Babes in the Wood*, for example, would be morbid for a toddler, but panders to the maudlin sentimentality of Victorians who liked Little Nell and thought dressing small girls up as beggars picturesque.

Of the three, it is Kate Greenaway who is perhaps best remembered – another artist of this era caught between a genuine childlike quality (she said, 'I hated to be grown-up, and cried when I had my first long dress') and the demands of an adult audience. She is also the only one I recall from my own childhood. We had a copy of *The Language of Flowers* on the bookshelves, with its secret world of signs: a yellow chrysanthemum for slighted love; lady's slipper for 'win me and wear me'.

Born in London to a working-class family in 1846,

Greenaway's mother was a busy dressmaker. While she was in the shop, Kate's childhood was spent wandering around Islington in the care of her big sister, watching *Punch and Judy* and street magicians. They used to play a game called 'Pretence' in which they would mimic the fancy shoppers. Her doll collection was her great pride – Dutch, wax and wooden. She had a favourite called 'One-Eye' and another called Gauraca that was four foot tall, and which she dressed in her brother's cast-offs.

Greenaway's early career was spent illustrating greeting cards, until Evans saw her manuscript *Under the Window*. On its publication in 1879 it became a bestseller. Soon Greenaway was famous for her doll-like children in quaint short jackets, smocks, pinafores, mob caps, and straw bonnets. Her mother's daughter, Greenaway would stitch these clothes herself before posing young models in them, creating an incredibly influential look ('Greenawayisme') that very much appealed to liberal Arts and Crafts mothers; they called themselves 'The Souls' and clamoured to dress up their children in nostalgic pantaloons. Her illustrations spoke to the contemporary cult of childhood innocence. With Liberty & Co. mentioning her in its adverts for muslin frocks, her game of 'Pretence' came to strange life.

Greenaway met the famous art critic John Ruskin when she was thirty-six and he was sixty-three, and their subsequent relationship dominated much of her adulthood. Ruskin had previously been in love with a nine-year-old girl, Rose La Touche, and it seems likely that

Greenaway's pictures of sweet children clutching roses in *Under the Window* encouraged him to start their correspondence. Greenaway considered herself plain – her father nicknamed her 'Knocker' because when she cried she looked like their door-knocker, and she filled her student notebooks with reassuring phrases like: 'Beauty is but skin deep.' Flattered by Ruskin's attention, she was soon exchanging hundreds of letters with him. Ruskin championed her work for showing 'the infantine nature in all its naïveté, its gaucherie, its touching grace, its shy alarm, its discoveries, its ravishments, embarrassments, and victories'. But he also led her on and could be caustic, as in his criticism of her illustrations for *The Language of Flowers*: 'they look as if you had nothing to paint them with but starch and camomile tea.'

John Ruskin had problems with adult female bodies – his biographer, Mary Lutyens, has suggested that his marriage to his first wife, Effie Gray, was unconsummated because he was disgusted by her pubic hair – and his flirtation with Greenaway also carried disturbing undertones. As the years passed, it seems she drew more to please him than any audience of children. Many of her letters to him are illustrated with the languorous 'girlies' he so enjoyed gazing at. In a letter from July 1883, he even tried to persuade her to undress one of her illustrations further:

> *WILL you – (it's all for your own good!) make her stand up, and then draw her for me without her hat – and, without her shoes, – (because of the heels) and without her mittens, and*

without her – frock and its frill? And let me see exactly how
tall she is – and how – round.
   It will be so good of – and for – you – And to, and for – me.

His cousin and companion, Joan Severn, got to the letter before Greenaway and pencilled underneath: 'Do nothing of the kind! – J.R.S.'

My favourite Kate Greenaway illustrations are those for the poet Robert Browning's *The Pied Piper of Hamelin* – their talents combine, somehow, to make the most perfectly Victorian picture book imaginable. Browning's realistic details make the pestilence vivid:

> Rats!
> They fought the dogs and killed the cats,
> And bit the babies in the cradles,
> And ate the cheeses out of the vats,
> And licked the soup from the cooks' own ladles,
> Split open the kegs of salted sprats,
> Made nests inside men's Sunday hats.

It is another book that stages a confrontation between anarchy and authority. Blame for the plague lies with the 'dolts' of the corporation, and the mayor is memorably brought to gross life:

> Nor brighter was his eye, nor moister
> Than a too-long-opened oyster,
> Save when at noon his paunch grew mutinous
> For a plate of turtle green and glutinous . . .

The Pied Piper himself – 'tall and thin, / With sharp blue eyes, each like a pin' – is promised a thousand guilders, but then refused his payment when the greedy adults of Hamelin remember they could instead spend it on council dinners with 'Claret, Moselle, Vin-de-Grave, Hock'. They are punished for this by the removal of their children, who are seduced by the musician:

> And, like fowls in a farm-yard when barley is scattering,
> Out came the children running.
> All the little boys and girls,
> With rosy cheeks and flaxen curls,
> And sparkling eyes and teeth like pearls,
> Tripping and skipping . . .

No one but Greenaway could illustrate such an eerie and beautiful scene. She decelerates her tempo to a picture per line, then a picture for a single word ('tripping') – the children dance forth in slow motion, their arms raised like puppets' or zombies' arms.

In many versions the Pied Piper leads the children, like rats, into the waters of the Weser river to drown. It is a tragedy of adulthood; of the failure of parental responsibility. But in this version the Piper leads the children into a mountain's mouth, and Greenaway adds something remarkable and additional to the text – a picture of the Paradise that lies inside. It is a sentimental idyll of peacock-bright sparrows and pretty, blushing youths wearing Kate Greenaway smocks, dancing hand-in-hand around the blossom trees. A revolution of innocents. A butterfly's ball.

A SPECIMEN PAGE OF MISS KATE GREENAWAY'S WORK.

From the "Pied Piper of Hamelin." (F. Warne & Co.)

It would be possible to argue this book is on the side of children rather than adults, with the Pied Piper a liberator, freeing them from their corrupt parents. By that reading, this is a dangerous image that suggests the overthrow of old hierarchies.

Except. Greenaway illustrated *The Pied Piper of Hamelin* entirely under Ruskin's guidance, as an attempt to please him. This last scene, which shows the celestial garden, and which he said perfected the story 'while it changes it into a new one', obsessed him, and he supervised her on every figure and pose. The Piper is a cipher for Ruskin himself: artist and choreographer, 'girlies' clinging round his lap. He even wrote: 'I think we might go to the length of expecting the frocks to come off sometimes – when it was very warm? You know.'

How could Greenaway ever hope to draw Ruskin his heaven? He was never satisfied. 'I *know* the Paradise is bad' she apologized in a letter to him, even as it was sent to the publishers. In later years, she stayed devoted as he slid into senility. Just a year after Ruskin passed away, in 1901, Kate Greenaway died of breast cancer, after silently suffering in abominable pain until it spread into her lungs. It was the beginning of the twentieth century; the thickest fog in years.

Greenaway could not have known, but, just a month later, Beatrix Potter would privately print 250 copies of *The Tale of Peter Rabbit*. For all the nineteenth century's obsession with childhood, it would take a mischievous bunny to make the leap (the hop?) into the modern picture book.

2. 'Ourselves in fur'

On animals in clothes

Randolph Caldecott's picture book *Baby Bunting* (1882) has no text beyond the short nursery rhyme:

> Bye, Baby Bunting!
> Father's gone a-hunting,
> Gone to fetch a Rabbit-skin,
> To wrap the Baby Bunting in.

The illustrations fill out the story to comic effect. Caldecott shows the father failing at hunting, and finally reduced to going to the shops to buy a rabbit skin. We then see Baby Bunting enjoying their present, crawling on all fours in a cute long-eared rabbit suit. But after the rhyme ends, we turn the page to see an additional image that, like the Paradise that Caldecott's fellow 'Triumvirate' member Kate Greenaway painted for *The Pied Piper of Hamelin*, adds a very different dimension to the text. It shows the mother and her rabbit-wrapped toddler on a country walk, passing a cluster of real rabbits.

In his marvellous essay on Caldecott, Maurice Sendak writes: 'I'd give anything to have an original drawing of that baby! – Baby is staring with the most perplexed look at those rabbits, as though with the dawning knowledge

that the lovely, cuddly, warm costume she's wrapped in has *come* from those creatures.' It is indeed an astonishing moment: is the baby suddenly aware of the pain of others? Of guilt?

Clothes are a marker of civilization. But they are also Adam's curse – the cover for our shameful nakedness; consequence of our sin. The picture is shocking, because it reveals what picture books so often carefully evade: the things that human beings do. Rabbits are a symbol of innocence because they are prey animals, almost defenceless. We, on the other hand, are apex predators.

There have always been animal stories. Stories are another way we exploit creatures – they are our meat, our clothes, our shelters, our guards, our transport, our workers, our company, our metaphors. The anthropologist

Claude Lévi-Strauss suggests that humans have long known animals are not only 'good to eat' but 'good to think'. Early religious stories often treat animals with a sense of awe. Egyptian gods have the heads of the lion or falcon. But by the time Aesop, by tradition an African slave, began to tell his fables in the sixth century BC, some of us had begun to feel comfortably superior. In his tales, animals are simple signifiers for human characteristics – the tortoise slow and steady, the peacock self-regarding, the wolf a tyrant – and they are all put on earth to illustrate our points. G. K. Chesterton describes them as less like animals than 'pieces in a game of chess'.

By the eighteenth century, animals were moving into the nursery, via moral tales such as Dorothy Kilner's *The Life and Perambulations of a Mouse* (1783) or Sarah Trimmer's *Fabulous Histories* (1786) about a family of robins. Understandable, perhaps, as another of the things we do to animals is to tame them: we domesticate them; overpower them; make them obey. We also tame children. The similarity between these two processes does much to explain how common animals have become in picture books, especially farm animals or pets. We make these creatures walk upright, like circus ponies. We put Anubis in mittens and a sweater and use him to teach three-year-olds how to behave. Maisy Mouse uses a zebra crossing. Peppa Pig goes to the dentist. Pip the rabbit forgets to ask for the toilet, wets himself and has to change his pants.

The first truly famous clothed animal in picture books is Beatrix Potter's Peter Rabbit. A descendant of both Carroll's White Rabbit and Brer Rabbit, the trickster of African-American folklore popularized by Joel Chandler Harris, he is a kind of hybrid. Half tame but still half wild. In illustrations, Peter is sometimes upright, sometimes on all fours like his true cunicular self. He is liable to lose his small blue coat and shoes when he is most vulnerable or foolish, as if his claims to semi-human status slide away. His father was put in a pie by Mrs McGregor (the original 1901 edition contains a picture of this, with a faint, blond toddler waving his fork in anticipation), and Peter is in danger of the same fate. But by a sleight of hand, the book doesn't turn small readers vegetarian. Instead, by making us see the world from Peter's angle – as the novelist and critic Alison Lurie notes, 'the vantage point in her exquisite watercolours varies from a few inches to a few feet above the ground, like that of a toddler' – the child becomes Peter, the vulnerable hero. The farmer, with his long white beard, shaking his fist and rake, seems to stand for all grown-ups, while Peter, greedy for mischief and radishes, is every child.

Beatrix Potter's brilliance is in the path she walks between sentiment and savagery. *The Story of a Fierce Bad Rabbit*, supposedly one of her stories for babies and originally printed on a strip of paper and sealed with a ribbon, is one of the most morally harsh. A rabbit takes a carrot from another rabbit without saying 'please', scratching him in the process. He has his whiskers and tail shot off by a man with a gun. The end. Is the human somehow an agent of divine retribution? *An eye for an eye and a tail for a carrot.*

Potter would boil dead birds to get a better look at their skeletons, so her beasts are anatomically correct, and she doesn't deceive us as to their diets. Subtle hints of humanness, rather than softening her characters' behaviour, often make that behaviour more sinister by introducing an element of premeditation. Jeremy Fisher's butterfly sandwich or roasted grasshopper with ladybird sauce are more grotesque for their preparation. The fact that the fox, Mr Tod, lives in a house in his skull-strewn wood, with a lock on the door and a carving knife that twinkles in the moonlight, makes for a darker nightmare. Mr Jackson, Mrs Tittlemouse's uninvited guest, is all latent violence, pacing down her passageways muttering 'Tiddly, widdly', wiping his mouth with his coat-sleeve, devouring the littlest creepy-crawly people. The gobbling of Jemima Puddle-Duck's beloved eggs by puppies is made much darker by the fact that they were 'saving' her from the fox in that familiar, last-minute dash of popular fiction. In *The Tale of Squirrel Nutkin*, even the squirrels are complicit in slaughter when they offer the owl Old Brown, in exchange for nuts, three fat mice, a fine mole and seven minnows as a blood sacrifice.

It is on the uneasy border between human and animal where Potter works; where she reminds us that we live.

Despite her love of nature, Beatrix Potter (1866–1943) spent most of her life a tamed thing, kept in dull, expensive isolation on the top floor of a house in South Kensington, without any friends her own age. London's rows of houses shut her in like 'great frowning hills'. She had long bouts of illness and tiredness. Her journals are chilling in their depiction of something close to psychological abuse – at nineteen her father took her out on a rare trip to an exhibition and her hat blew off. 'He does not often take me out,' she wrote. 'I doubt he will do it again for a long time.'

It has been suggested there is something autobiographical in the attractive but comfortless doll's house of *The Two Bad Mice*, with its lobsters, ham, pudding and pears that won't come off the plates though they are 'extremely beautiful'. But at least Beatrix and her brother Bertram had many pets over the years, which animated the nursery floor and gave Potter much-needed friendship: dogs, rats, various rabbits (including Benjamin H. Bouncer, who she would walk on a lead, and Peter, who could drum a tambourine), a tortoise, bats, lizards, a ring snake called Sally, an owl, a kestrel, a jay (which killed a bat 'in a disgusting fashion'), a frog called Punch, Mrs Tiggy the hedgehog, mice called Hunca Munca and Xarifa, various snails including Lord and Lady Salisbury, and a robin without tail feathers (that she later freed).

Potter was thirty-five before her first book came out in 1901. It began as a letter to the sick child of her former governess. *The Tale of Peter Rabbit* was rejected by six publishers before she self-published it – but in doing so, she moved the picture book into the twentieth century. One innovation was that the books were, unlike the heavy, expensive nursery books of that time, small enough to fit into a child's pocket and only cost a shilling, but she was also original in other ways. Potter began the movement away from poetry anthologies towards our contemporary model of picture books as single, original stories. She also pioneered ideas like deliberately including at least one difficult word in each book, in order to help expand the children's vocabulary. (I am looking at some now and trying to guess which words. I suspect: ponderously, disconsolately, alacrity, conspicuous, indigestible, conscientiously, soporific.)

Soon she had 'real' publishers – Frederick Warne & Co. Norman Warne understood her meticulous eye, buying doll's house furniture for her to base her drawings on in *The Two Bad Mice*, for example (because doll's house furniture isn't quite the same as full-size furniture), and they entered into a lively correspondence. She also led the way in children's book merchandising. After a disastrous episode in which her books were pirated after her publishers forgot to register the US copyright, Potter became very attentive to patents. If Peter Rabbit is the first great twentieth-century picture book, Potter's business acumen set a precedent that would be keenly followed – by 1904 she had already designed a Peter Rabbit doll and board game, with painting books and pottery coming swiftly afterwards. Exploiting family links with the textile business, she also sold the rights to her images for nursery wallpaper and fabrics. (Interestingly, though, despite her eye for an opportunity, she did prevent Walt Disney from producing an animated movie in 1938, saying: 'it seems that a succession of figures can be joggled together to give an impression of motion. I don't think the pictures would be satisfactory . . . I am not troubling myself about it.')

In July 1905 Potter became engaged to Norman Warne, with whom she had finally found companionship and love. He died a month later, of lymphatic leukaemia. Despite this tragedy, Potter had been given a taste of freedom from her parents, so was not prepared to give it up.

Soon afterwards, she bought Hill Top Farm in the Lake District. When she arrived it needed a great deal of work – apparently, amongst other problems, housing ninety-six rats. The struggle with daughterly duties and grief continued. In his famous essay on Potter, Graham Greene labelled 1907–9 her dark period (and when Greene says that, it must be seriously dark) – but she had more air to breathe, at least. It was at Hill Top she invented Samuel Whiskers, Jemima Puddle-Duck, Pigling Bland, the Flopsy Bunnies, Timmy Tiptoes, Ginger and Pickles, Tom Kitten and those 'two disagreeable people' Tommy Brock and Mr Tod.

Hill Top is now run by the National Trust. If you visit the property with its hearth, dark rooms and crooked panes that turn the sheep wobbly, you can see some of the objects she amassed there over the years: tiny leather gloves; early examples of christening beakers and plates decorated with her characters. There are also two wonderful Caldecott prints that Potter chose from the many in her father's possession after his death, one of which depicts small children watching a trap in a snowy field, rapt as a bird edges closer.

Beside it, though, is a tableau of heartbreak. The doll's

house Potter bought because she could not bear to throw away the furniture Norman Warne gave her.

At school I was Mrs Tiggy-Winkle in an infant play, which might explain why it is still my favourite Beatrix Potter book. Graham Greene praises the way Potter can 'draw a portrait in one sentence', singling out: 'My name is Mrs Tiggy-Winkle; oh yes if you please'm, I'm an excellent clear-starcher.' I didn't have to wear her prickles, just a pinafore and cap, and had to fuss with washing and an iron, anthropomorphized all the way to human.

In *The Tale of Mrs Tiggy-Winkle*, clothes are not optional extras for birds and beasts, who must in fact get dressed in their furs and feathers each morning. A little girl called Lucie encounters a hedgehog called Mrs Tiggy-Winkle, and watches while she irons Cock Robin's bright waistcoat and launders Sally Henny-penny's yellow stockings. There are also Tabby Kitten's mittens, Tom Titmouse's starched shirt-fronts, the woolly coats of lambs, and a moleskin waistcoat. Every animal, it seems, obeys some kind of sumptuary law. They are not naked and free but, like obedient children, wearing their pressed, smartest best. Lucie seems disgusted by even the smallest flashes of animal she perceives in Mrs Tiggy-Winkle, who is figured as lower class, with her brown, wrinkled, soapy hands.

In the end, the shawl and frilled cap melt away. The separation between humans and animals returns, and the hedgehog flees from Lucie in naked fear. In the girl's eyes Mrs Tiggy-Winkle seems utterly diminished by losing her clothes. She shrinks and dulls, losing her title, role, security and magic, as she is exposed as 'nothing but' a hedgehog. Except she isn't. There is a bracketed addendum from Potter in smaller type:

> (Now some people say that little Lucie had been asleep upon the stile – but then how could she have found three clean pocket-handkins and a pinny, pinned with a silver safety-pin?
>
> And besides – *I* have seen that door into the back of the hill called Cat Bells – and besides *I* am very well acquainted with dear Mrs. Tiggy-winkle!)

It is a conjuring trick that reminds me of the poet John Keats' idea of negative capability (described in a letter as 'when a man is capable of being in uncertainties, mysteries, doubts, without any irritable reaching after fact or reason'). Potter allows the child to be both doubter and dreamer, realist and believer, quite aware of what 'some people' say, but choosing, nonetheless, the storyteller's better truth.

Beatrix Potter was soon much imitated. By 1929 another writer eighteen years younger, Alison Uttley, along with illustrator Margaret Tempest, had also created a world of animals in clothes called *The Squirrel, the Hare and the Little Grey Rabbit*. Uttley grew up in rural Derbyshire, a childhood lightly fictionalized in her stunning children's novel

The Country Child (1931) with its descriptions of a lost world of stirring milk with hazel wands, collecting cowslips, haymaking, posies and candlelight. Extremely bright, she obtained a scholarship at Manchester University to read physics, going on to teach. She began to write when her adored (or, at least, smothered) son John was sent to boarding school, in order to keep telling him tales. When her husband committed suicide soon afterwards, aged forty-seven, by drowning himself in the river Mersey (nagged to death, his relations believed), it also became a matter of financial necessity. She went on to be so successful that she could afford to buy a Brueghel, although her diaries show a woman who found it hard to be happy. Uttley hated comparisons with Beatrix Potter, who she felt was a jumped-up illustrator and a 'rude, old woman', whereas she believed herself to be a great storyteller. 'A spinner of tales', as it says on her grave. The diaries are also full of bitchiness about Margaret Tempest, who she never forgave for being paid more on their first collaboration (calling her 'a humourless bore').

If Potter dealt in bad rabbits, the Little Grey Rabbit is saintly – the critic Frances Wilson has called her a 'flopsy domestic goddess'. In the first book, her servile relationship to Squirrel and Hare is deeply uncomfortable. In her dress with 'white collar and cuffs' she looks like their maid, and like a maid must sweep, dust, lay the table and make tea from daisy heads before they get up. Hare is bored of lettuce for breakfast and sends the Little Grey Rabbit out in search of carrots at risk of her life (at one point a sack is thrown over her). In a scene I find absolutely chilling, the Little Grey Rabbit asks Wise Old Owl how to grow carrots, and in order to get the answer is told, to her horror, that she must give up her tail. She bravely asks that he 'be quick', before he cuts it off with 'one bite of his strong beak' and wraps the stump in a cobweb.

Why does she make this sacrifice of her own body for the conceited Hare's whims? When she returns to the house, he even labels her lack of tail 'disgraceful' and makes her blush and hang her head. By the end of the story, after she saves Squirrel and Hare from a Weasel, they apologize and offer her a breakfast of toast and coffee in bed, but she tells them: 'I like to work, and I don't want toast and coffee.' Whether she is modelling the behaviour of a housewife or a servant, the message is that some people can be violated and exploited, and this is their choice.

The name of your first pet plus your mother's maiden name is famously your 'porn-star name'. Mine is Twinkle Cranshaw. Twinkle was a goldfish, christened after my favourite magazine and bought in a clear plastic bag at a fair. Classic first pet.

Naming pets is, for small children, often the best part of having them. My son has three fish – little platies: one the colour of a clementine, one dirty gold, one the lapis blue of a beautiful old pot. He has called them Bing, Bang and Bong (or as his father and I know them, after taking them on a few 'trips to the vet': Bing II, Bang IV and Bong I). He also has a pet woodlouse, Dank, who he looks for in our garden most evenings in the summer.

'Hi, Dank,' he says, his voice warm with recognition, when he identifies the one under the log who is definitely Dank.

He has always adored animals and would like a bigger pet, although I have seen him with next door's cats and can already guess how that would play out – years of painful unrequited love as the cat refuses to play with him, then leaps the fence. I am also generally uneasy about the enslavement of animals into service as human companions. In my experience it never worked out well. My cat, Pizza, scratched my baby sister so badly he had to be put down. My hamster, Anastasia, died of obesity in a cage that always smelt pissy however often we changed her sawdust. We had a budgie, named Peter Scudamore after my father's favourite racing jockey, who we hoped would sit on our shoulders and chatter. Instead he flew every day to the mirror and stayed, banging his head against the glass.

The question of whether humans can bring happiness to animals leads us to *The Story of Babar*, produced by the artist Jean de Brunhoff in 1931, and based on a bedtime tale his wife Cécile made up for his two small sons. Many consider it a pivotal moment in the genre due to the intricate, graceful colour images that often spread across two pages; the interplay of text and image, which seems to set the standard. Brunhoff wrote and illustrated six more Babar books before he died of tuberculosis, aged only thirty-seven.

The Story of Babar begins with a little elephant born in the Great Forest to a loving mother. By the fifth page

she is dead, shot by a hunter who now runs towards Babar to catch him.

The birds are fleeing off the page, the monkey has hidden his head in a bush, but Babar stays on top of his mother's slumped body – two straight lines of tiny, dark tears pouring downwards from his face. It is perhaps the most upsetting image in the history of the picture book – the total grief of a child losing a parent, mixed with our fear that something terrible might happen to the child. It is the precursor to the death of Bambi's mother, or the bit we fast-forward through at the start of Pixar movies like *Finding Nemo* or *The Good Dinosaur*.

If Babar's mother's death feels unnecessarily cruel, it is worth acknowledging the argument of the critic Bettina

Hürlimann that the books were written by a dying young father, who contracted TB in his early thirties, and who saw the books as a way of speaking to his children after his death. This is a moving thesis, and one that might explain why Babar's grief never seems to get processed. Babar runs to a town. It looks like Paris and is filled with white people like those who killed his mother. What could be more frightening? Yet almost the first thing he thinks to himself on arrival is: 'What lovely clothes they have got!' He meets a rich old lady who notes his desire and gives him her purse. Within hours Babar is kitted out at a huge department store with a shirt, collar and tie, a 'delightful' green suit, a bowler hat, shoes and spats. Rather than mourning, Babar is an example of a creature who can live in the moment and take life's pleasures where he can (mainly from the wardrobe). Brunhoff shows us that the worst can happen, yet life goes on.

Unlike all the other clothed animals in picture books, we actually see how Babar procures his shirts – we are given a kind of genesis myth. Indeed the whole book is on some level *about* clothes. When he meets his cousins, Celeste and Arthur, the first thing Babar does is dress them (their reward is a trip to the patisserie). When he returns to the Great Forest all the elephants shout: 'What lovely clothes!' It is on the basis of his suit, symbol of how much he has learnt, that he becomes King – or should I say, he is offered the crown. Published by an imprint of Condé Nast, the book is so obsessed with style that some have wondered if this is coincidence.

It has also been argued, by critics such as Ariel Dorfman

and Herbert Kohl, that Babar's clothes symbolize the colonial project. To be upright, bathed, and dressed in the best French tailoring is to be given the right to rule, and in the third book, *Babar the King*, Babar swiftly turns the Great Forest into 'Celesteville' (named after his Queen), a European-style city with straight boulevards, a port, a library, formal gardens with a touch of Versailles about them. He also constructs a 'Palace of Work' and a 'Palace of Pleasure', introducing a capitalist system whereby these activities are strictly separated, and where an atomized workforce must now each take a specialized job – shoemaker, mechanic, clown, road sweeper, soldier. A prize-giving is initiated to make the children compete against each other.

For the inaugural garden party a small choir sings the 'Song of the Elephants' in what sounds suspiciously like a mock-African tongue: 'PATALI DIRAPATA / CROMDA CROMDA RIPALO / PATA PATA / KO KO KO'. But none of the elephants present, it is noted, know what the words mean any more: their native language has been extinguished. As in Scottish author Helen Bannerman's notorious picture book *The Story of Little Black Sambo* (1899), where the names of the South Indian boy's mother, Black Mumbo, and father, Black Jumbo, piece together to mock their language as primitive nonsense (mumbo-jumbo), the colonized culture is reduced to funny noises.

I find it almost impossible not to take pleasure in the images of the Babar books – they are so delicate and original. Pictures like the wedding party, or the hot-air balloon sweeping over the coast and blue sea (Brunhoff's rapturous blues!) are pure delight. My own favourite pages, for their sheer surreal strangeness, show a host of angelic elephants labelled LOVE, HOPE, JOY, GOODNESS, chasing away the curious bestiary of SLOTH, COWARDICE, STUPIDITY and DISEASE (the latter is like an earless hound, whose mouth is a hose spraying toxic particles). But enjoyment makes the reader, like Babar when he covets the lovely green suit, complicit. I feel the impulse to defend the artist who was so absurdly talented and died so horribly young, but I also have to recognize that he had internalized the values of his society, and those values were problematic.

This is a fantasy of Africa as *terra nullius*, where the white people meet only elephants and monkeys. It is not until the second book, *Babar's Travels*, that there is an encounter with blackness, after Babar and Celeste land on an island with natives described as 'savages' and 'cannibals'. Babar fights them. There is a double-page spread of wounded and dying black bodies. It is both technically beautiful and actually evil. Babar shows us these things can co-exist.

The critic Adam Gopnik, writing in *The New Yorker*, tried to justify the books on the grounds that they satisfy us with 'the child's strong sense that, while it is a very good thing to be an elephant, still, the life of an elephant is dangerous, wild, and painful. It is therefore a safer thing to be an elephant in a house near a park.' But is it really? Any child would know that this is nonsense. Gopnik might feel more secure living in a house near a park, but to suggest that it's the case for *any living being* is to erase our differences. And why is safety what we aspire to anyway? The promise of 'protection' is what the powerful historically use to keep us in line.

Sadly, the Babar books are propaganda for the powerful. They say we must dress properly, work hard and internalize their values. We must respect those in charge, even when they kill our parents.

Animal stories, though, have always relied on a kind of essentialism – call it speciesism – that is so close to racism as to perhaps make such ugliness inevitable. When Arthur N. Applebee, writer of *The Child's Concept of Story* (1978), asked school children to describe the personality traits of various animals, he found they were surer of the characters of those they knew exclusively from books: brave lions, sly foxes. Once they moved on to animals they had actually met, like dogs, their answers became less definite and more nuanced. English-language children's books constantly urge readers to trust their instincts and rely on snap judgements; to make assumptions about creatures based on their physical appearance – sneaky rats, proud peacocks, mischievous monkeys, sly snakes, wise owls with their spectacle-eyes (although I was assured at a falconry class once that owls are actually poor at problem-solving, and in India they symbolize foolishness). We're encouraged to judge the genus by our very flawed, human projections on to them, and then the individual by the genus.

The very worst example of this is the picture book published during the Third Reich, *Trust No Fox on his Green Heath and No Jew on his Oath* by Elvira Bauer and

Philipp Rupprecht. It was published by Julius Streicher, who would later be found guilty of crimes against humanity at Nuremberg, under his Stürmer-Verlag imprint in 1936. This foul book teaches children how to 'identify' Jews by their appearance and names. It compares them to foxes who are similarly 'seen everywhere as a pest' and were associated in Germany with both sneakiness and spreading rabies. The book's 'Jews' are also depicted next to crows – birds thought to carry out the Devil's work. As war spread many adults wanted to return to the certainties of their childhood: a world where the wolf is always evil; a lamb reproachless.

The antidote to this, though, is Munro Leaf and Robert Lawson's *The Story of Ferdinand*, published the same year, about a bull who doesn't want to compete in a Madrid bullfight, preferring to smell the flowers. It was released three months after the start of the Spanish Civil War by Viking Press, although they considered holding it back until 'the world settles down'. By 1938 it was a surprise bestseller in the United States, beating even *Gone with the Wind*. Its seemingly pacifist message unsurprisingly resulted in it being banned in Spain until after Franco's death. In Nazi Germany, Hitler ordered it burned.

It also irritated Ernest Hemingway enough for him to write a short story called 'The Faithful Bull' that starts: 'One time there was a bull whose name was not Ferdinand and he cared nothing for flowers.' Hemingway ends his tale with a hideous formulation that has the ring of propaganda: 'the man who killed him admired him the most.'

*

The thirties and forties were busy times for picture books. Publishers began launching their first children's divisions – the Caldecott Medal was established in 1938, the first Puffin Picture Book was launched in 1940, and Simon and Schuster's Little Golden Books started in 1942. Although the Second World War briefly caused cutbacks in materials, it also seemed to increase demand for books relating to the innocent, carefree world of childhood. Afterwards, the post-war baby boom expanded the market, as did the establishment of things like children's library services in the UK. Publishers began thinking carefully about marketing. Who was buying these books? Not the children. How to please the reader, and yet also appeal to the buyer: the mother, the teacher, the librarian?

In the history of picture books, the writer Margaret Wise Brown is, like Beatrix Potter, one of the great heroines. Her youth was also marked by a love of nature. She claimed to have grown up 'along the beaches and in the woods of Long Island Sound', burning leaves, or collecting shells and cherries. She had a full menagerie of quirky pets (squirrels, a collie dog, a hare, hens, fish, a robin who returned every spring, and, apparently, thirty-six rabbits) and after she obtained her first book deal, she asked a flower-seller to deliver a whole cartful of flowers to her New York apartment. Brown was striking: tall, with green eyes and hair the colour of timothy grass (her nickname was 'Tim'). She had scandalous affairs both with men and with a glamorous older woman known as Michael Strange. She died tragically young of a blood clot, after showing a nurse how well she felt by kicking up her legs in a can-can.

Brown deserves to be remembered as someone who brought an incredible sophistication to picture books in this exciting period of growth. Refusing to dumb down, her texts drew inspiration from Gertrude Stein, and the art suggestion she sent to illustrator Clement Hurd for her famous *Goodnight Moon* was a reproduction of Goya's 'Red Boy' ('Manuel Osorio Manrique de Zuñiga') with his green cage of finches and magpie on a lead. She began writing at a time when most books were printed in a basic palette of cyan, magenta, yellow and black. At first she worked with Lucy Sprague Mitchell on the influential 'Here and Now' series, which aimed to produce more realistic juvenile literature that rejected fantasy in favour of the ordinary surroundings of the children, and was aimed squarely at kindergarten teachers. She worked hard doing research; taking children to the docks and the zoo to see what they noticed, and testing early material on classes. From these basic beginnings, her confidence in her vision began to grow.

After some early successes, Brown was lobbying to pay illustrators more and to use blended colours. She began writing under several pseudonyms for various publishers, often penning four titles a year for Little Golden Books alone – a series produced in bulk and sold in drug and department stores, making picture books affordable to many families for the first time (their idealistic sales slogan was 'Books and Bread'). After the Second World War, as new printing techniques became possible, Brown was at the forefront of innovation, hand-making prototypes: pages cut into animal shapes, novelty add-ons like a watch or a mouse on a ribbon, pull-out posters, glow-in-the-dark paint.

The publisher Brown worked for as an editor, William R. Scott, Inc., experimented with some of the earliest 'textural' books, precursors of all the modern board books with fuzzy and bumpy patches, including a wordless rag book called *Cottontails* (1938) with buttons, bows, beads and rabbits' tails Brown helped stitch on. In 1940 Brown's contemporary, Dorothy Kunhardt, had a hit for Simon & Schuster with the similarly textural *Pat the Bunny*, with its peekaboo rag and shiny mirror ('Now YOU pat the bunny') and its witty advertising campaign that declared: '*For Whom the Bell Tolls* is magnificent – but it hasn't any bunny in it.' Ever competitive, Brown's own book with illustrator Garth Williams, *Little Fur Family* (1946), soon took this idea of tactile books for small children even further. The tale of a little fur child, who lives in a cosy home, venturing out into the world and encountering other creatures, its first print run had a cover made of real rabbit skin. The book retailed at $1.75, but there was also a limited-edition mink version at $15. Ursula Nordstrom, Brown's editor, later said that she knew the book would be hugely successful when she received a letter from a mother whose boy had held his copy open at dinner and attempted to feed it.

(The moths in Harper's warehouse loved it too, so the next edition was fake fur.)

Margaret Wise Brown is best known, as it happens, for two other books about rabbits, both illustrated by

Clement Hurd. The first, *The Runaway Bunny*, published during the Second World War in 1942, is based on a Provençal French ballad, 'Les Métamorphoses', in which a lover promises their beloved that 'if you change into a fish / I will change into an eel / And I will eat you', and that even if they die 'I will change into dust on your grave / And I will wed you'. It is an unsettling poem that hints at an obsessive, abusive relationship, but Brown thought children would enjoy its catchy 'if you, then I' formula. She decided, inspired by child psychology, to base it on the stage at which children want to make their first independent steps, but are also filled with separation anxiety. In it, then, a young rabbit plots myriad ways to escape, and his mother tells him how she will find him. Brown wrote it on a skiing holiday, scrawling it down on the back of a ski receipt, before Clement Hurd was commissioned to do the images.

Between them they created something that is an oddly changeable text, depending how you hold it to the light. Hurd's pink-eyed white rabbits have strangely emotionless faces, on which we can project our own ambiguous feelings. Sometimes the book is deeply moving and reassuring – the bunny says he will become a bird, the mother says she'll be the tree he comes home to (a bunny-shaped tree is drawn with its branches as open arms). The child is testing the limits of adult love, finding that there are none.

On other readings, the mother's promise to become a fisherman if her child turns into a fish sounds like a threat. Even if the little bunny becomes a boat and sails far away, he will be unable to escape his mother's influence. She will be the wind and 'blow you where I want you to go' (her face appears in a cloud, like a vengeful god's). Childhood is figured as a state of being under surveillance. In the end the little bunny submits to the impossibility of escape, settling for a carrot in his burrow.

The date of publication seems relevant. Perhaps in 1942 the idea of a son setting off alone on adventures overseas held a different charge. Perhaps all mothers wanted to believe that they would still be with their children, somehow, wherever in the world they went.

Harper marketed the book heavily to parents and grandparents, placing ads in consumer magazines suggesting it was the perfect Easter gift, and printing postcards for bookshops to slip in bags. They must have realized this book's appeal was not so much to the child as to the adult's ego: their romantic sense of themselves as ardent protector. The book is the precursor to Sam McBratney and Anita Jeram's *Guess How Much I Love You* or all those books called things like *I Love My Daddy* or *Mummy is Magic*, which I suspect are mainly bought by the named adult. Brown's book was an enormous hit.

In Brown's second classic, *Goodnight Moon*, the rabbit is much less rabbity. It only, in fact, became a rabbit in editorial meetings, as Clement Hurd, who was again illustrating, felt he was better at drawing them than children. It has become a cipher for a child, who lives not in a burrow but a vast, off-kilter room, surrounded by the trappings of civilization – art, a doll's house, mittens, a comb, a telephone. She says goodnight to each object in what feels like a ritual to induce comfort. Originally, apparently, the book was meant to end 'goodnight cucumber, goodnight fly', which would have made it funnier, but the revision was clever – this book is not meant to induce giggles or flights of fancy, but yawns. In a way, like *The Runaway Bunny*, it's also a book meant to make the child submit.

Goodnight Moon is picture book as lullaby; as bedtime routine; as the parent's little helper. A lullabook. At the time, this was ground-breaking, and puzzled many with its lack of story, but now it is much mimicked (even spawning the enormously successful adult parody *Go the F**k to Sleep* by Adam Mansbach and Ricardo Cortés). Even the weirdest line of the original – 'goodnight nobody, goodnight mush' – feels sleep-inducing, like the babblings of a child hallucinatory with tiredness.

It's also considered one of the first examples of an animal in a picture book as simply (in critic Margaret Blount's phrase) 'ourselves in fur'. So far is the rabbit removed from animality that even the picture of a cow's udder on her wall has been blurred to avoid offence.

We barely think of the rabbit as a rabbit at all, just a little girl so sweetly tucked in with her rabbit suit.

Brown's animals are sugared versions of ourselves: paler, gentler. In *The Color Kittens*, illustrated by Alice and Martin Provensen, and another of Brown's hit books, the protagonists are called Brush and Hush – soft, smoothing words. These kittens are dressed as little workmen, and their work is explicitly human: art, artifice, dream, the creation of fantasy realms where Easter eggs dance on tiny legs.

But like Beatrix Potter (who boiled up corpses to see their anatomy better) Brown did not anthropomorphize animals in life – she loved to hunt, keeping pace with hounds on foot. Her biography by Amy Gary describes a scene in which Brown hunts deer with her lover James Stillman Rockefeller Jr (also known as 'Pebble') and then, when the kill is cut open, holds the 'still-warm heart in her hands', radiant as Snow White's mother.

Picture all the children in their bedrooms stroking the cute and cosy copy of *Little Fur Family*, its cover peeled from the rabbit's flesh and sinew – an estimated 15,000 having been skinned to produce the 50,000 copies. We are so young when we learn not to ask about the suffering of others. If we feel warm and safe, it is best not to think too hard about how and why. It is best to tell ourselves different stories.

In *Little Fur Family*, the fur child finds a tiny version of itself. Kisses it and sends it on its way.

As rabbits become more anthropomorphized, we might notice something else happens. Unlike Peter, or Pooh's friend Rabbit, the rabbit in *Goodnight Moon* is a girl. This gendering of creatures is something that becomes increasingly noticeable over the history of picture books.

When my son was born and I first ventured into Mothercare's clothes department, I realized that almost everything in the world has now been segregated into masculine or feminine categories. Girls could count, for example, on all the pastels (except blue) plus purple and hot pink, while red and green were siding with the XY chromosome. In terms of territory, the boys most definitely got the sea, including whales, crabs, anchors, navy stripes and all who sailed on it. They also got space – astronauts and monsters fight the male corner. Oh, and they got the past (dinosaurs) and the future (robots) and all modes of transport. In the animal kingdom, the tigers, bears, crocodiles, sharks, lions and monkeys – anything viewed as strong, meat-eating, cheeky or violent – had clearly been recruited for the boys while the meeker, smaller, milkier creatures such as mice or kittens were with the girls. They also had allies in butterflies, ponies and birds.

Yellow and elephants, like Switzerland, were neutral.

Miffy is a girl, her frock as simple as the sign on a woman's toilet cubicle.

Is Miffy the very essence of rabbit? Or the least rabbity rabbit of all?

Born in 1955, she could be viewed as the progenitor of the 'first experiences' genre, which has since bred like you know what. Trina Schart Hyman railed against the ubiquity of these stories in 1986, claiming that 'every other picture book' was now about animals doing human things. Research seems to bear her out – a 2002 review of around a thousand children's books found that over half featured animals, but fewer than 2 per cent depicted animals realistically. Hyman continues: 'It says, Henrietta's First Trip to the Dentist. Well, Henrietta's a racoon, you know, with Nikes and a little pink dress on. And the dentist is a rhinoceros ... Why couldn't Henrietta be a kid and the dentist be a real dentist?' The answer is perhaps that we feel animals create a distance that makes the mundane more magical; the morals easier to swallow. But, interestingly, the University of Toronto's Ontario Institute for Studies in Education (OISE) found that, in a 2017 study of nearly a hundred children, those who heard a story about human characters sharing became more generous, while those who heard the same story with an anthropomorphized racoon actually became more selfish. If we want our picture books to give children moral lessons, perhaps we do need more real kids and real dentists.

For good or ill, though, the genre became big business with Dick Bruna, whose titles include: *Miffy goes to the Zoo*, *Miffy in the Snow*, *Miffy at the Seaside*, *Miffy's Birthday*, *Miffy at the Playground*, *Miffy in Hospital*, *Miffy and the New Baby*. In the book I have in front of me now, *Miffy at School*, there is no narrative arc beyond her conformity with the school's routine. In a crowd of other girl bunnies who share her face, Miffy learns to get up early, to sit for the register, to do her sums. Parents and educators have bought over 85 million of these books, hopeful of inducting their children into such adorable obedience.

Bruna apparently had the inspiration for Miffy when he saw a little rabbit in the dunes with his one-year-old son, Sierk, so told him a story. Early on she had floppy ears – it took until 1963 to refine her into the rabbit we now know, and an English translator, Olive Jones, to come up with her name Miffy (she had originally been Nijntje, a shortening of Konijntje – 'little rabbit' – in the Dutch). Soon though, influenced by Matisse's collages, Bruna refined Miffy into a minimalist masterpiece.

Every book has only 12 pages, each 16 x 16 cms. Each page has one picture and four lines of verse. Bruna uses a thick black line and – like the De Stijl movement – a pared-back palette of poster paints (in his case: black, white, red, yellow, blue, green and orange). Miffy always looks directly towards us. Her rabbit-ness is distilled to this: two ears and a cross for mouth and nose.

Everything is similarly stripped to a kind of Zen simplicity – Bruna told Lisa Allardice, in an interview for *The Guardian*, that making Miffy sad could take days as he might begin with five tears then try to cut back as much as possible: 'At the end I have one big tear, and that is the saddest tear you can have.'

In this minimalism, Miffy also ushered in something

else. She is picture book character as logo. Almost no one can recall a Miffy story, yet we all know her from the endless product – placemats, mugs, aprons, greeting cards, lamps, totes, magnets. In this she was so ahead of her time, her image seems startlingly modern. Bruna followed Beatrix Potter's lead and took the merchandising to another level – especially merchandising to young girls. He led a quiet life, its only real narrative in the later years being his legal case against Sanrio for their imitation of Miffy, Hello Kitty, whose habit of wearing pink particularly disturbed him (he claimed it was 'not a proper colour'), and whom he sued for copyright infringement when they introduced Kitty's friend Cathy, a familiar-looking rabbit.

Miffy is an animal who is no longer an animal. In one remarkable book in the series, called simply *Miffy*, Bruna even tells the story of her birth, where an angel appears in Mrs Bunny's garden and says she shall have her wish for a baby granted. Miffy, like Jesus, is born utterly innocent, untainted by animal sin (her parents clearly not at it like rabbits). She isn't made of fur or pie-meat. She is a brand, a proto-emoji. Caldecott's bunny girl cleansed of guilt.

Bruna talked of wanting to leave space for young children to project on to her, and however hard we look, Miffy just stares straight back at us with those two dots.

She is the face in our mirror, and we look *so* cute.

3. I Know How a Jam Jar Feels

On greed and pickiness

One of the tastes of my childhood is the taste of golden plums. They were a Polaroid yellow; the colour of late evening sunshine. We had a plum tree in the garden and at harvest time it would chirp with little tits and finches pecking at their sweetness. We had to shoo them away. My dad often led school harvest assemblies, where I recall him standing in his suit before hay bales, piles of apples and glazed bread wreaths; bread mice with currant eyes. The children of the village had to make up harvest boxes for the elderly, then knock on doors with the gifts. Ours always contained a couple of tins, a packet of biscuits, a dozen golden plums. We'd have plum crumble for weeks.

When we first moved to Peckham and I was pregnant, my husband bought me a golden plum tree. It grew as Gruff grew. In his third year there was a bumper harvest, but then when I bit into the first fruit expecting a nostalgic reverie I noticed something – a kind of reddish scum around the stone. Tiny blood-coloured specks. I spat the plum back into my hand and broke open another one. Something tiny and pale pink squirmed there, like a maggot or a baby's smallest finger.

Later I discovered the problem was plum moths. The blight has recently spread through gardens at great speed, no one is sure why. The dark scrim was shit. My golden plums were full of hungry caterpillars.

The first transgression involves fruit. Usually we think of an apple. This was possibly a misunderstanding or a pun on *mălum*, a Latin word which means evil, and *mālum*, which means apple. In fact, scholars now suspect the fruit in the Garden of Eden was a pomegranate or a fig. As children, we understand the story instinctively. We want to put everything in our mouths, after all: dandelion stalks, pebbles, Lego bricks, earwigs (I ate an earwig as a toddler and said it was 'nice and crunchy' when they tried to drag it from between my teeth). We want to taste and know.

One of Laurie Lee's earliest memories, in *Cider with Rosie*, is of his sisters stripping the fruit bushes and cramming his mouth with berries whilst he sits like 'a fat young cuckoo'. Ripe fruit, hung luminous in the trees by the road or on barbed-wire bushes, has always been a dangerous temptation. Children might, after all, gobble up a glut of it when the adults aren't looking; make themselves sick. The historian Siân Pooley has written of how in the nineteenth century 'death by fruit' was frequently recorded as the reason for infant deaths. It was probably superstition, but born out of the fact that some berries are poisonous. That, and the sweetest fruit is often the most corrupt, only hours from bruises, collapse or rot. Filthy fingernails pick it off the floor.

Christina Rossetti's 1859 children's poem *Goblin Market* plays on this fear. It is about two girls, Laura and Lizzie, who hear the calls of goblin merchants to 'come buy' their dizzying array of fruits:

> Apples and quinces,
> Lemons and oranges,
> Plump unpeck'd cherries,
> Melons and raspberries,
> Bloom-down-cheek'd peaches,
> Swart-headed mulberries,
> Wild free-born cranberries,
> Crab-apples, dewberries,
> Pine-apples, blackberries,
> Apricots, strawberries;—
> All ripe together
> In summer weather,—

Longing for these fruits but with no money to pay for them, Laura offers the goblins a lock of hair and a single tear as payment. Lizzie reminds Laura about Jeanie, a girl who ate the goblins' bounty, then pined away and died at the beginning of winter. But Laura doesn't listen to her sister's warning, laughing: 'to feel the drip / Of juice that syrupp'd all her face, / And lodg'd in dimples of her chin'.

My children are fruit crazy. Both my first child, Gruff, and my small daughter, Cate, demolish punnets in moments; a mango in minutes. Truly, their faces are 'syrupp'd'. And they love books about fruit. They adore *Handa's Surprise* by Eileen Browne, for example, and know by heart who takes the 'sweet-smelling guava' from Akeyo's basket (the ostrich), or the 'spiky-leaved pine-apple' (the giraffe).

But for us, I think, the platonic ideal of fruit – the longed-for, perfect fruit of our fantasies – will always be the radiant collages of Eric Carle in *The Very Hungry Caterpillar* (1969), made by layering hand-painted tissue paper on to white board. Cate was bought a stuffed Very Hungry Caterpillar when she was born, one of the many pieces of *Very Hungry Caterpillar* merchandise that fill the bookshop tables these days, and we call it the 'Caterpillar'. Sometimes we call *her* the Cate-rpillar. I wriggle it and she giggles. When I read it she grabs at the die-cut holes with her fingers: one apple, two pears, three plums, four strawberries, five oranges, and then the finest prize of all, a huge lurid irresistible slice of watermelon.

You remember the watermelon.

Until he was six, Eric Carle lived in upstate New York – the Big Apple – with his parents, who had migrated from Germany. He has recalled it fondly in his talk 'Where Do Ideas Come From?', delivered to the Library of Congress, Washington D.C.: 'I remember kindergarten there. I remember a large sun-filled room with large sheets of paper, fat brushes and colorful paints. I remember that I went to school a happy little boy.'

Then, in the mid-1930s, his mother got homesick. Persuaded by Carle's grandmother that the post-First World War years of chaos had finished, she decided the family should move back to Stuttgart, even as others were moving away. It was a terrible decision. Carle's new school was a dark room with narrow windows; a teacher who beat him with a bamboo stick. In an interview with Leonard S. Marcus, Carle has spoken of how, in Germany at that time, it was thought that children needed to be 'broken in', and a 'free-spirited little American kid' especially so.

War broke out, and Carle's father was drafted into the German army. He would spend eight years as a Russian prisoner of war and return home devastated. In his absence Carle struck up an important relationship with an art teacher, Herr Krauss, who showed him artists banned by the Nazis – Picasso, Braque, Matisse – when he was supposed to teach 'realism, naturalism, Aryans with flags waving'. He even dared to call the Nazis 'charlatans' and *Schweine*. But Carle also saw things a child should not see. He and his mother began to spend many hours sheltering in their cellar. He told *Newsweek*: 'It was scary at times. The nearest bomb was maybe 20 feet away, and it shook the house . . . when it passed, my mother took my head and put it in her lap. I will never forget that.' When he was only fifteen the German government conscripted him to dig trenches on the Siegfried Line, where: 'The first day, three people were killed a few feet away. None of us children – Russian prisoners and other conscripted workers. The nurses came and started crying.' He was left with post-traumatic stress disorder.

Another episode also occurred that left its impact on Carle when he had to be evacuated. Foster families were allocated by default, with slips of paper handed out to children telling them the name and occupations of the people who would take them in. At the train station, Carle's friend Herman complained that Carle had been given the best family – he would be living with a baker, and be sure to get lovely fresh bread. He moaned so much that Carle gave in, and they swapped addresses.

But Carle got the nicest family in town. The cruel baker made Herman sleep in an icy, unheated room under his eaves. He got no extra bread at all.

Since it was first published *The Very Hungry Caterpillar* has sold a copy every minute. It has been translated into over 30 different languages and sold over 20 million copies. But it started with holes. 1969. Carle, back in America, bored and punching holes in paper.

Carle wondered if a children's book could use holes. It was not, in fact, the first time an artist had come up with this idea – Peter Newell's *The Hole Book* in 1908 shows a boy fooling around with a gun and accidentally discharging it, sending it through clocks, hats, cats, hives and a cake – but Carle's concept was perhaps more conducive to the nursery. His first idea was 'A Week with Willi Worm', about a green bookworm, but his editor, Ann Beneduce, was not persuaded – particularly as it didn't have an ending. They tried to think of something better until Ann said, 'Caterpillar!' and Eric said, 'BUT-TERFLY!!' The holes, they decided, would be holes in fruit. For a while they couldn't find a manufacturer who could guarantee the holes would line up, until Beneduce found a printer in Japan.

Hunger is a kind of hole. A nothingness that some-how demands of you. A void that brims with hurting.

In his *Paris Review* interview, 'The Art of Fiction No. 299', Eric Carle observed:

> My publisher and I fought bitterly over the stomach-ache scene in *The Very Hungry Caterpillar*. The caterpillar, you'll recall, feasts on cake, ice cream, salami, pie, cheese, sausage, and so on. After this banquet I intended for him to proceed immediately to his metamorphosis, but my publisher insisted that he suffer an episode of nausea first—that some punishment follow his supposed over-eating. This disgusted me. It ran entirely contrary to the message of the book. The caterpillar is, after all, very hungry, as sometimes we all are. He has recognized an immense appetite within him and has indulged it, and the experience transforms him, betters him. Including the punitive stomachache ruined the effect. It compro-mised the book.

That spread we all love is the essence of plenitude – the triangle of watermelon, the salami *and* sausage, Swiss cheese with holes in it like a Hanna and Barbera mouse's dream, a vast pickle to enliven the palate, a cupcake *and* chocolate cake with a cherry *and* cherry pie, a lollipop of swirling blue and yellow like the roof of a circus tent, a cone of sunrise-coloured ice cream. It is designed to stimulate every type of hunger. 'I'm licking my lips,' my son says when he anticipates a meal. 'Yum yum, I'm licking my lips.'

It is also, in a way, a depiction of the dream of America.

In his autobiography *The Art of Eric Carle*, he writes about how at the end of the war he worked as a file clerk in the US denazification department, getting access to the American army kitchen where he swiped 'peanut-butter sandwiches, lumps of butter, cubes of sugar, leftover bits of steak' for his family. Imagine Carle's anticipation when he saw that feast laid before him.

Carle's friend Herman was no greedier than we all are when we look at those pictures. Brought up under rationing, having experienced the real physical pain of a clenching, empty stomach, what boy would not fantasize about food, or hope for more where he could find it? Herman did not deserve his fate at the hands of the baker.

And Eric Carle, hungry for success and publication, letting his editor persuade him against his instincts, is punished disproportionately too: 'This disgusted me.'

He has betrayed his friend somehow.

The Very Hungry Caterpillar wasn't Eric Carle's first picture book. He had previously worked on *Brown Bear, Brown Bear, What Do You See?* (1967) with the author Bill Martin Jr, at a time when Carle was art director of a New York advertising agency. Bill Martin Jr was inspired to collaborate with Carle after seeing an advert in which he had drawn a big red lobster.

Advertising is the semiotics of desire. That spread of food in *The Very Hungry Caterpillar* is, in many ways, like an advert too. The fantasy that indulging ourselves might in fact better us is, of course, a fantasy advertising sells us. It is based on the view that the pursuit of individual pleasure might create a better world, that you can have what you want without consequences. It is easy to see why *The Very Hungry Caterpillar* has come to be seen as a metaphor for capitalism. A young East German librarian once told Carle: 'This book would never have been published here. The caterpillar represents a capitalist. He bites into every fruit, just takes one bite and he moves on, getting fatter and fatter. He's exploiting everything.' The critic Anthony Lane even suggested, in *The New Yorker*, that it is 'a matchless parable for the entrepreneurial right'.

That's not exactly fair, though. The caterpillar is a child. He still has so much growing and changing to do. Isn't childhood the one time that we do not need to be responsible? As an adult, I find it hard to eat a beefburger or drink a flat white or buy a tub of air-freighted blueberries without waves of guilt. A dim, ugly sense of consequence. I have eaten of knowledge and the fruit tastes bitter. But can a child not eat and drink of the world's delights without this burden?

Hunger does not always improve our lives. Hunger for home can lead your husband to a prison cell. It can lead to your fifteen-year-old son digging trenches and getting PTSD. This 'immense appetite' within us is a dangerous thing. But in *The Very Hungry Caterpillar* Carle wants to say not always. Not inevitably. Some children crave warm, fresh bread and there is no price to be paid. Some children gorge on fruit and become beautiful.

*

I have often observed other parents in the park teaching their children vague, general words, as if imagining specific vocabulary is too much for them to take in. Look: a birdy. Look: a pretty flower. I don't know, perhaps some of the parents aren't even familiar with the names themselves: that it is a great-tit or a bluebell. If the specific words aren't passed on, in the end they vanish into obscurity, disappearing as catkin, lark and minnow did from the *Oxford Junior Dictionary* in 2015 (to be replaced by 'cut and paste' and 'broadband').

But children seem to me to have an enormous appetite for nouns. At only slightly over two, my son could name an absurd number of animals. He collected their tiny plastic replicas with a desperate obsessiveness, constructing whole continents on the coffee table and updating me daily on new mammals he had discovered he needed: a mandrill, a tapir, a tamandua (a genus of anteater that sadly could not be located for purchase). Like Adam in the Garden of Eden, Gruff seemed determined to name every creature in the world; to bring it into being. But also, of course, this appetite for words came from wanting to name the objects of his desire: other, different plastic toy animals.

Desire is very specific. Amongst my daughter Cate's first half-dozen words are not bird and flower, but *owl* and *daisy*. She will not be appeased by a cuddly parrot or buttercup. In the kitchen she cries for fruit: *nana* she says, or *melon, melon, melon*. I cut a slice like the one the caterpillar eats: neon and dripping. She crushes fistfuls into the tiny, ravenous hole of her mouth, juice sluicing everywhere.

*

The sixties were the start of a golden period for picture book talent, with many of the greatest writers and illustrators – Dr Seuss, Eric Carle, Judith Kerr, Maurice Sendak – hitting their stride during this decade. Judith Kerr's *The Tiger Who Came to Tea* (1968), published the year before Carle's masterpiece, is also a book about hunger. The tiger famously eats everything – he empties the table, the saucepans, the cupboards, the fridge and the taps. If the English ritual of afternoon tea – a teapot, buns, cake, biscuits and tiny crustless sandwiches (cucumber, perhaps, or ham, with lots of butter) – is considered by those who indulge in it to be a high point of civilization, the tiger's desire is uncivilized. He is pure hunger and selfishness. But unlike the caterpillar, his appetites do him no harm: he just gets to eat until it has all gone and he leaves.

Kerr, of the same generation as Carle, also had her war story. Born in Berlin, she was the daughter of Julia Weismann, a pianist and composer, and Alfred Kerr, a revered German-Jewish theatre critic who openly criticized Nazism, mocking Hitler in witty verse. In 1932 he was put on a Nazi death list. After being tipped off that his passport was going to be taken, he disappeared, fleeing in the night for Prague. In 1933, on the day Hitler took power, the rest of the family fled too. Judith Kerr was nine.

It was the right decision, but the family's lives soon became difficult. All Alfred Kerr's payments for his writing were stopped and his books were publicly burnt in 1933 in the Opernplatz, under Goebbels' direction. There was a reward placed on his head for anyone to capture him, dead or alive. As refugees, the family stayed briefly in Switzerland and France, but always felt pursued until they finally settled in Britain. Even there, staying in Bloomsbury, they found themselves in the middle of the Blitz and Judith Kerr said: 'My main preoccupation at that point was a conviction that I wouldn't live to be eighteen.' However, Kerr never positioned herself as history's victim. Her fictionalization of that period, the novel *When Hitler Stole Pink Rabbit*, frames the flight across Europe as an adventure from the child's perspective, and in interviews she has said: 'I wouldn't have missed it for anything!'

After the war Kerr wanted to go to art school full-time but, being a refugee, money was still a problem. Instead she obtained a trade scholarship in the studio of a textile manufacturer, which allowed her to go to art school part-time. When this finished, she got a job as a script reader for the BBC for twelve years, of which she has said: 'It seems extraordinary to me now that for about twelve years of my life, I did not do any serious drawing.' She only began drawing again after she had her first child, a daughter called Tacy. Kerr recounts that when Tacy was 'two going on three' they often went to the zoo to see the animals, and afterwards, 'She would say imperiously, "Talk the tiger."' The story Judith Kerr told her daughter became her first picture book, *The Tiger Who Came to Tea*.

So, the tiger is a tiger from the zoo, anthropomorphized to delight a little girl in a tale that included 'everything she liked'. Except . . .

People have argued that the tiger is like the war. In early sketches, Kerr drew him with a top hat and cane, perhaps making a mockery of Europe's civilized veneer; its powerful gentlemen with their brute intentions. The tiger turns everything upside down; leaves the middle-class family suddenly stripped of basics. In the ultimate barbaric act, tearing up the social contract, he pours hot tea into his mouth directly from the teapot (an image that led to calls for the book to be banned for setting a dangerous example to children).

There are parallels, too, between the beast and the child's-eye view of Hitler in *When Hitler Stole Pink Rabbit*. In that book, when the children imagine the Nazis con-fiscating everything, they picture Hitler playing Snakes and Ladders with their games compendium and snug-gling little Anna's pink rabbit. Like the tiger, Hitler is figured as greedy, taking everything for his own pleas-ure and leaving their cupboards bare. The poet Michael Rosen, famously, also said that given Kerr's history the tiger seemed to him suggestive of the Gestapo. 'Judith knows about dangerous people who come to your house and take people away. She was told as a young child that her father could be grabbed at any moment by either the Gestapo or the SS – he was in great danger.'

It's a fascinating idea, though it recedes slightly when you look again at the pictures and realize that the tiger is not forbidding. Although he is not a cartoon tiger, he has sweet, slant eyes and a warm smile. He never shows teeth, only a bright tongue, and says excuse me and thank you and waves goodbye. Before the tale even begins – on the title-page spread – we see Sophie riding his back under a benignly grinning sun, effectively quelling any

anticipation of menace. Children are reassured that nothing in the pages that follow will frighten them. Also, the little girl is hugging his beautiful orange coat as he looks around the kitchen for more food, her fingers stroking the whiskers around his mouth. His tail cups her face as he empties the taps. Unless Kerr is making the same point as Sylvia Plath in her poem 'Daddy' ('Every woman adores a Fascist . . .'), the Gestapo analogy won't quite stick. Judith Kerr herself put it nicely: 'I don't think one would snuggle the Gestapo, even subconsciously.'

Still, the war is certainly a presence in the book. The academic Rebecca Bramall is convincing when she argues that Sophie's father's return echoes men's return from the war. The shift from the empty cupboards of a family on rations to the utter luxury of a restaurant supper 'with sausage and chips and ice cream' would have had a different resonance to adults reading it aloud in the 1960s, as would the images of the family walking beneath street lamps, to readers who remembered blackouts.

But you will have heard other theories too. *The Tiger Who Came to Tea* is remarkable as a children's book, it seems to me, for the sheer number of theories that circulate around it. It can feel like there are more interpretations of its 'meaning' on Mumsnet than there are about Coleridge's 'Kubla Khan' in academia. One theory suggests that as *The Tiger Who Came to Tea* was released in the year of Enoch Powell's Rivers of Blood speech, the tiger is the foreign 'other' who the family fear will take everything if he is invited in. The tin of Tiger Food, in this reading, re-establishes the divide between 'them' and 'us'. I'm unsure about this racist slur against Sophie and her mummy, given Kerr's own status as an immigrant, but perhaps there is something in the association with foreignness. Certainly, the tiger is conspicuously removed from his natural landscape and reduced to English social rituals. Perhaps he is homesick, and comfort-eating to fill that hole that can't be filled.

Then there are the theories about the mother. She is lazy, and with her daughter concocts a fantasy about a tiger to explain away her empty cupboards. She is an alcoholic, and the story is her frankly unbelievable excuse for drinking all Daddy's beer. She is having an affair, and the tiger is her lover in metaphorical disguise.

Aren't mothers often figured as tigresses too? Perhaps he is an expression of her id; the instinctual drive to pleasure usually suppressed by housewives.

The critic Jenny Uglow's reading of the text doesn't go quite so far, but suggests it is a story about seduction – of the mother who defers to this display of appetite; the complicit daughter with her arms wrapped around him. The tiger, she says, 'harks back to the fatal fascination of the alarming mysterious stranger, like the devil in ballads and fairy-tales who arrives without warning and disappears with equal suddenness, and who is longed for as well as held in awe.'

Judith Kerr says 'sometimes a tiger is just a tiger', but sometimes writers can tease us. If he was just a tiger he would eat the girl and her mother before he worked out how to use a tap.

Anyway, tigers in stories are never just tigers. They are human inventions, puppeted by human longings: the longing to skip a bath, stay up late, eat hot salty chips, find meanings.

One thing I do think is clear from their attitude to greed is that Carle and Kerr are both anarchic spirits. In both books unspoken laws are broken about what should and shouldn't happen, about actions and consequences. Wayward appetites are supposed to leave everyone in tears. Instead, in these books, they are energizing. They lead to beautiful rainbow-coloured butterflies and sophisticated café suppers.

Other famous picture books are more judgemental.

In Martin Waddell and Helen Oxenbury's *Farmer Duck*, the boxes of expensive chocolates the farmer eats on his bed while duck does all the hard labour are a sign of his immorality, leading to a coup. In Janet Burroway and John Vernon Lord's *The Giant Jam Sandwich* the vast treat (so outsized 'eight fine horses' have to drag the bread to the picnic cloth and trucks have to dump on the butter) is not constructed for pleasure, but as a death trap for wasps, who deserve their comeuppance for making a beeline towards the bait. Maybe Carle and Kerr are so beloved because they take our children's first and funda-mental source of sensual pleasure and say: enjoy.

But what makes us take pleasure in something? Some books teach us new names for our desires. Stories can even shape them. Bee Wilson has written of how in 1936, a young psychologist exiled from Nazi Germany, Karl Duncker, carried out a taste experiment on children at a London nursery school. He asked their teacher to read the story of a heroic field mouse called Mickey who loathed a 'sour and disgusting' substance called hemlock, and thought nothing more delicious than 'maple sugar'. Afterwards the children were given some white choco-late powder and told it was 'hemlock', and some horribly bitter valerian and told it was 'maple sugar'. Sixty-seven per cent said they preferred the 'maple sugar'.

Our tongues often taste the story not the flavour.

To Duncker, this evidence of suggestibility was chill-ing. The ease with which a child could be manipulated into changing their tastes mirrored the ease with which

Nazi propaganda had manipulated the population of Germany into changing their morals. Two years later, aged just thirty-seven, Duncker killed himself.

I have certainly desired foods I have never tasted, because the story seemed to me so delicious. For me Enid Blyton was about skip-reading from picnic to picnic – the large hams, crusty loaves, red radishes, slabs of butter, melt-in-the-mouth shortbread, tinned pineapple and, most of all, lashings of ginger beer. It didn't matter that I hadn't tasted ginger beer and had previously dismissed radishes as tasting of stale water, I wanted them feverishly. And what young reader hasn't dreamed of Roald Dahl's Everlasting Gobstoppers or J. K. Rowling's Fizzing Whizbees?

In picture books, though, only a few equal *The Very Hungry Caterpillar* in terms of actively making me hungry. *The Lighthouse Keeper's Lunch* by Ronda and David Armitage is one – in a charming story (though one slightly marred by the fact that Mrs Grinling exists only to provide her husband with delicious lunches), Mr Grinling is fed at the lighthouse every day via a basket sliding down a piece of rope, until the seagulls start to sabotage his food. Who can blame them? For a sample lunch contains mixed seafood salad, cold chicken garni, sausages and crisps, lighthouse sandwiches, peach surprise, iced sea biscuits, drinks and assorted fruits. I'm sure few children know what 'garni' means, or what a lighthouse sandwich might contain, and yet mouths start to salivate at David Armitage's radiant paintings. My children also adore *Full, Full, Full of Love* by Trish

Cooke and Paul Howard, where Sunday lunch at Grannie's house includes 'buttery peas, chickens and yams, macaroni cheese, potatoes and ham' as well as biscuit and gravy, collard greens, apple pie, vanilla ice cream and peach cobbler with raspberry sauce; *Possum Magic* by Mem Fox and Julie Vivas, with its list of Australian delicacies with transformative powers: pavlova, lamingtons, Vegemite sandwiches.

Similarly, as a child I was hypnotized by the meals in Russell and Lillian Hoban's masterpiece *Bread and Jam for Frances* (1964). Frances, based on a little girl who lived next door to the Hobans, is depicted as an anthropomorphized badger. She was originally intended to be a vole but Russell was apparently persuaded by his editor, Ursula Nordstrom, that it would be too difficult to create a likeable vole. The first book, *Bedtime for Frances*, was illustrated by Garth Williams, but after that Russell's wife Lillian took over.

There is a scene in *Bread and Jam for Frances* in which Frances is eating bread and jam again when her friend, another little badger called Albert, gets out his packed lunch:

'What do you have today?' said Frances.
'I have a cream-cheese-cucumber-and-tomato-sandwich,'
    said Albert.
'And a hard-boiled egg and salt shaker.
And a thermos of milk.
And a bunch of grapes.
And a tangerine and a cup custard.'

He tucks a napkin under his chin, arranges his lunch neatly, and then – after cracking his egg and sprinkling salt on the yolk, takes a mouthful each of sandwich, egg and milk until they all come out even.

It's Albert's delight but also his seriousness, I think, that moves me. How much it all matters to him. The first time I read it to my son my voice broke a little.

I think it's the reason my last meal would be tapas.

Bread and Jam for Frances also means so much to me because it is tangled up with another memory.

In the village of Edgworth, social life centred around a building called The Barlow Institute which had a bowling green, playpark, cricket pitch and cricket club behind it. At weekends parents would watch cricket while kids went on the swings, and I would sip Britvic 55 (pineapple juice with a slight fizz of bubbles) and eat Scampi Fries while balls puttered towards the boundaries of the pitch. Thursday night was the men's night out, when the cricket club became the meeting place of the local chess team (of which my dad was captain). He would psyche himself up beforehand, listening to 'Eye of the Tiger' in our living room. He drank pints of mild that they ordered in just for him. Once I heard him tell my mum about a typical conversation – the men had been deciding if they'd rather have sex with their wives or eat a pie. Apart from him, apparently, they all opted for the pie.

Whilst he was out, my mum usually had her friend Sheena over, and they would write plays for the WI.

They rehearsed in The Barlow Institute on Wednesday evenings, and on that night Dad would babysit. He made it feel like a treat. My sister and I sometimes made a 'Mr Men window', laying out every single Mr Men book in a giant square grid – from *Mr Small* to *Mr Tall* – and then playing games to pick which one Dad would read. (It was a family joke that my dad was like Mr Skinny, because he was very thin and when he put on weight he would just get a little pot-tum.)

My dad, who, as it happens, was also called Albert, would then make us something called a 'secret supper'.

Our bungalow was open plan, with a little partition between the dining room and the kitchen. My mother, always verbally inventive, called this the 'interim-agreement' and I believed for many years this was its actual name, rather than the term for a transitional agreement between nations like, say, the Israeli-Palestinian Oslo Accords. Dad would pull a curtain across it so as not to spoil the surprise, then out of our vision he would assemble the 'secret supper'. Bring it out like a magician producing a rabbit.

A cream cracker with a smidge of shrimp or chive Primula spread. Three grapes. A Jaffa Cake. Apple slices with cheese. Two Iced Gems, like tiny bobble-hats knitted by elves in the night. One cube of unmade jelly.

A little bit of everything seemed to me the perfect meal.

Looking back, my dad ate with the tastes of a child. He ate like a child who had been forced to masticate nothing but over-boiled cabbage and could finally choose for himself. Certainly, my Grandma Pollard was an atrocious cook, although in her larder, beside the blue-tit-pecked milk bottles slushy with ice, she did always keep something sweet like ice-cream roll. It was my Grandad Pollard, though, whom my father was really rebelling against – the mean, joyless Methodist who thought nothing my dad ever did deserved praise. My dad loved processed meat, so would frequently reward himself with a tin of hot dogs or pâté on toast (the cheap sort squeezed out of a plastic sausage) for breakfast. He often indulged himself with a paper bag full of Liquorice Torpedoes. Every night of his adult life – *every single night* – my father would wake up at 1 o'clock, tiptoe into the kitchen, open the fridge and make himself a banana milkshake. He would have a small Flake to accompany it, the kind you get in boxes for 99s. He would then brush his teeth and tiptoe back to bed, an adult in thrall to the idea of the midnight feast.

But he was also, like many children, a fussy eater. Because being picky is the other side of getting to choose. It's choosing not to. It's refusing to put something in your mouth, because you're old enough to realize you don't have to. They can't make you. And the dinner table is a place where you have power.

He wouldn't eat vegetables. He left them at the side of his plate when Mum cooked them. Or, I tell a lie, he only liked mushrooms, onions and butter beans. He would eat no fruit except bananas (he ate one briskly every break time at school, as his concession to health).

*

Bread and Jam for Frances by Russell and Lillian Hoban is a book about pickiness. The opposite of Albert's delight in every flavour is Frances's monomania. She likes bread and jam because if she knows what she is getting she is always pleased. Her opposition to other foods seems to be mainly textural – we discover this from the little songs she sings to herself about poached eggs and their '*funny little quiver*'. She, it is implied, is shivering like the eggs are. Such neophobia has a practical application in nature – children are right to be nervous of things they put in their mouth that are sloppy, squishy, tough, gritty or loose. It's a way of keeping them safe, and Frances only feels safe with food that is familiar.

Her parents decide to let her eat bread and jam exclusively, in a rather high-stakes game to see if she gets sick of it. But it's also a clever strategy, because if pickiness is about children claiming what power they can over themselves, her parents allow Frances that power. Instead of forcing string beans and veal cutlets down her throat with forks or threats, they give Frances what she wants until she discovers she doesn't want it. Until she skips with her rope and finds herself singing:

> *Jam for snacks and jam for meals,*
> *I know how a jam jar feels –*
> *FULL ... OF ... JAM!*

(As an aside, I am always interested in what parents do at bedtime when they arrive at a 'song' such as this. Do they simply read it aloud? Do they sing it? Do they make up a tune or use a well-known one and try and make it fit? I always put words to the same kind of repetitive, lilting, semi-flat tune I must have made up off the top of my head long ago for just this purpose, without really putting enough commitment into it, and the results are fairly disappointing.)

In the end two tears roll down Frances's badger cheek, and she asks if she may have some spaghetti and meatballs, then eats it all up. In the triumphant final scene, Albert asks her what she has for lunch, and she brings out a doily and a tiny vase of violets. She has tomato soup in a thermos, celery and a salt shaker, a sandwich filled with lobster-salad, carrot sticks and two black olives, plums and a miniature basket piled with cherries, and a vanilla pudding in a cup with a spoon.

Albert decides this is a good lunch, and I agree. It still delights me, because it is a book about the wonderful, various world. A world which has so much more in it than predictable sugars and bland white carbs. A world of pleasures that awaits if you only let yourself try.

Which brings me to *Green Eggs and Ham* (1960). It is perhaps, thinking about the profound pleasure I take from reading it aloud, one of my top ten poems ever. This is notable because I don't recall even reading a Dr Seuss book as a child, although I was vaguely aware *The Cat in the Hat* existed – Seuss's books weren't such a big thing in the UK in the 1980s. My love of him is not nostalgic – it's based on my complete admiration, as a fellow adult poet, for his genius. If anything, before my first child was born I was absolutely prepared to loathe him.

My head was full of garish, shouty movie trailers (Mike Myers, Jesus!). His presence on my Twitter feed was split evenly between articles about his racist cartoons and supposedly 'inspirational' quotes:

'Keep on shining' #DrSeuss

'Don't cry because it's over, smile because it happened' #DrSeuss

'You know you're in love when you can't fall asleep because reality is finally better than your dreams' #DrSeuss

'Only you can control your future' #DrSeuss

I mean, he sounded appalling.

In fact, to read about Dr Seuss is to discover a man full of complexities and contradictions. A shifting, ambiguous figure, who said 'kids can see a moral coming a mile off', yet somehow managed to write books that have been seized on as moral fables by everyone from environmentalists (*The Lorax*) to pro-life protestors (who use his slogan from *Horton Hears a Who!*, 'A person's a person, no matter how small'). A man who, during the war, drew caricatures of Japanese Americans as invading hordes and Africans with monkey-like features, yet who could write *The Sneetches*, a children's book about the evils of racist propaganda. *Oh, The Places You'll Go!* is so sentimental it is a popular gift for students graduating from high school in the USA and Canada, with a sales spike every spring. Yet it is also true that Seuss could be, as he claimed, 'subversive as hell'.

He was born Theodor Seuss Geisel in 1904, to a family of German immigrants in Springfield, Massachusetts. His father managed the family brewery, Kalmbach and Geisel (known locally as 'Come Back and Guzzle'), making thousands of barrels a year of porter, ale and lager. His mother had been a baker's daughter and would chant the names of pies, as she had done at the counter, to send her children to sleep: 'Apple, mince, lemon . . . peach, apricot, pineapple . . . blueberry, coconut, custard and SQUASH!' His childhood memories were largely happy, although an eighteen-month-old sister, Henrietta, died of pneumonia when he was three. He would always remember the sight of her tiny casket in the house.

When he was a teenager two shadows appeared. First, America entered into war against Germany and anti-German feeling began to run high, with frankfurters renamed 'hot dogs' and sauerkraut 'liberty cabbage'. Then in 1919 the Eighteenth Amendment was ratified and the family brewery doomed.

Prohibition was a time of forbidden fruit. Seuss grew to love drawing, inspired by comic strips like *Krazy Kat*. At Dartmouth College he regularly contributed to the humour magazine *Jack-O-Lantern*, but was banned after being caught swigging gin with friends in his room. In this genesis story, to continue to contribute, Geisel began signing himself off as 'Seuss'. (The pronunciation is usually anglicized, but he said that the correct, German pronunciation is to rhyme it with 'voice'.)

Seuss's real breakthrough didn't come until 1954. *Life* magazine ran an article that blamed high illiteracy amongst school children on all their books being too boring (they were typically primers about ordinary kids, like *Dick and Jane*, Seuss memorably summing them up as 'Dick has a ball. Dick likes the ball. The ball is red, red, red, red, red'). The director of education at Houghton Mifflin, William Ellsworth Spaulding, responded by compiling a list of the first words that early readers needed to recognize – or, as Seuss put it, 'the number of words that a teacher can ram into the average child's noodle' – and asking Seuss, who had already published a couple of picture books, to write a poem using them that children couldn't put down. Legend has it that Seuss found the first two that rhymed – 'cat' and 'hat' – and proceeded to write *The Cat in the Hat*.

It took him many months, though. Part of the problem was the words themselves. His article 'My Hassle with the First Grade Language', written for the *Chicago Tribune*, has a brilliantly funny passage about this – the words were 'thrillers . . . like *am*, *is*, *but*, *if*, *in*, *into*, *no*, *yes*. Words full of great adventure . . . like *milk* and *mitten* and *mop*'. He had been given a near impossible brief – to write a joyful, action-packed page-turner, whilst remembering to 'Repeat! Repeat! Taking care, of course, not to be boring.' There was also the problem of finding rhyming pairs. 'The list had a *daddy*,' Seuss notes. 'But it didn't have a *caddy*. I found myself snarling: "faddy, maddy, saddy, waddy".'

The result is a remarkable poetic feat. Poetry often works by using constraints – it is language pushed to its limits by imposing 'rules'. Poetries can be structured around alliteration, metre, rhyme schemes or syllable counts. Seuss uses these, but in *The Cat in the Hat* he was introducing a whole new form of constraint – a highly restricted vocabulary. There are parallels with the work of the French avant-garde movement known as OuLiPo, founded in 1960 by Raymond Queneau and François Le Lionnais, who invented forms like the Lipogram, which excludes certain letters, or the Univocalism where you are only allowed to use a single vowel (such as 'a' or 'u'). But Seuss's innovation is in a mainstream children's book a decade earlier. And the remarkable thing is that the constraint is never noticeable. The story – of that mysterious, dangerous cat and his minions, Thing One and Thing Two, descending on the house when Mother is away (a story so sinister and contrary to our current awareness of child protection issues that I am often reminded of director Michael Haneke's film *Funny Games* when reading it) – never feels forced or limited by the vocabulary. In fact, the book feels deliciously lawless, even though this is, to some extent, an illusion.

Maurice Sendak has memorably said that Seuss drawings 'all look like bowel movements' and the book is 'in the literal sense shitty', enacting a rebellion against the tyranny of toilet training before conceding that the mess needs tidying up. It is a poem bursting with anarchy that makes us long for the anarchy to be over (the parents reading it aloud feel themselves identifying with the anxious pet fish). It is a book in which anything might happen, yet one written under the pressure of incredibly tight linguistic laws. In *The Cat in the Hat*, Seuss manages to hold anarchy and authority in tension in a way that is part of his talent.

If you find that impressive, wait until you try *Green Eggs and Ham*, the result of a bet between Seuss and Bennett Cerf, his publisher, that Seuss could not better himself and write his next book using only fifty words.

Those fifty words are: a, am, and, anywhere, are, be, boat, box, car, could, dark, do, eat, eggs, fox, goat, good, green, ham, here, house, I, if, in, let, like, may, me, mouse, not, on, or, rain, Sam, say, see, so, thank, that, the, them, there, they, train, tree, try, will, with, would, you.

Fifty words! A book! It's impossible, yet *Green Eggs and Ham* is a story with a beginning, middle and end. It has genuine narrative propulsion. It's memorable. It's funny. It even achieves poetic scansion.

It's the tale of an unnamed character who looks a little like *The Cat in the Hat*, except his stovepipe hat is a rather dull black rather than striped like a barber's pole. He's also not a cat. More of a dog, loose-eared, a bit battered and jowly, with the air of a put-upon authority figure. But he has the same long, fuzzy step; the same identical eyebrows and lashed lids and tiny pert nose.

As the book begins, this character – let's call him Anon – is like anyone's exhausted parent, trying to read the newspaper. And then another, smaller, more upbeat little fur-fellow enters the book, standing on a strange beast's back, grinning, with a sign that declares: 'Sam I am.' (What kind of name is that, by the way? What a boastful confidence in his own existence!)

He proceeds to offer our unnamed protagonist, via a long mechanical arm, a plate of green eggs and ham. It is interestingly a kind of reversal of what usually happens in homes, where the grown-up offers the food and the small person refuses. This time, it is the grown-up who turns up his nose at a proffered dinner. However, as the yolks of the eggs are a vibrant algae colour and, it should be noted, the ham is also completely green, it could be argued that it is a meal no one in their right mind would eat. This is nothing like the Seuss-inspired recipe for green eggs and ham that Martha Stewart says 'is a fun meal idea your kids will love' (involving an arugula, basil and parsley pesto folded into scrambled eggs). Rather, this screams mould and twenty-four hours hunched over a toilet bowl. His proffered plate refused, Sam-I-Am spends the whole of the rest of the book wondering whether Anon would, perhaps, eat it if only the context was different.

It is a delight to read. The constant repetitions, particularly, as Anon gets angrier and angrier, and must list all the ways in which he does not want to try green eggs and ham are marvellous to perform aloud. The iambic tetrameter makes it roll along on the tongue with such momentum (an iamb is a basic 'foot' or unit of poetry which has an unstressed syllable followed by a stressed syllable. 'I **will**.' Each line here is made up of four iambs – 'I **will** | not **eat** | them **with** | a **mouse** / I **will** | not **eat** | them **in** | a **house**').

The work is a dialogue poem – an interesting form in itself. It means you've just worked yourself up into a peak of irritation when you have to cut back to the chirpy voice of Sam-I-Am. I can never get through it without giggling. Always a sign of the best books, *Green Eggs and Ham* has also become part of my everyday dinner table conversations with my son. I'm lucky that, so far, neither of my children are very picky, although Gruff has taken against leaves in all their guises, but whenever I want him to try something new I make up new questions: 'Would you eat it with a dog?'

'I would not eat it on a frog,' Gruff says, solemnly, poking a mushroom.

Because the moral *seems* to be that you can't know whether you will like something until you try it. Sam-I-Am is proved right, after all. Following a wonderful wordless double-spread in which fox, mouse, goat, Sam-I-Am and assorted others hold their breath as Anon raises a sagging green egg on a fork, he eats it and realizes it is delicious after all. Trying is shown to be the key.

But is this actually the meaning of *Green Eggs and Ham*, or is something darker at play? Is Seuss on the parent's side, helping us encourage our children to sample new foods, or is he satirizing our hysterical attempts at persuasion?

In some ways, I must admit, Sam-I-Am is a kind of over-zealous advertiser, selling his heavily adulterated foodstuffs which, frankly, must be full of E-numbers and colourings. (Look, you can even eat them in a car or in the dark! They might lead you to new friendships with mice and foxes! They taste of adventure and company!) He repeats his message, over and over, until the consumer gives in.

Do I want my children to learn that they should eat something that looks bad for you, just because a cute cartoon creature with catchy jingles repeatedly tells you so (I'm looking at you, Honey Monster and Tony the Tiger)?

Or could he even be a propagandist, of the kind Karl Duncker was reminded of when he persuaded children to go against their own taste buds? In many ways this is a tale about suggestibility. Sam-I-Am brainwashes Anon into embracing what he naturally reviles. What, in fact, he *should* reject. It ends with poison entering the bloodstream. Submission. Our unnamed protagonist obsequiously thanks Sam-I-Am as he cleans the plate of its grotesque fare.

Perhaps I am going too far, but there is something about the books of Dr Seuss, a kind of radical ambiguity, that allows people the space to project all sorts of theories. That's his great genius. And I am not going as far, at least, as the People's Republic of China, which in 1965 banned *Green Eggs and Ham* for its 'portrayal of early Marxism'.

There is one more book that belongs in this chapter. It is *In the Night Kitchen* (1970), by Maurice Sendak, one of his trilogy loosely based on children's psychological development in which *In the Night Kitchen* is about the toddler, *Where the Wild Things Are* the preschooler and *Outside Over There* the pre-adolescent. Each of them, he notes, is about 'one minute's worth of distraction' and 'begins with a child in rage'. *In the Night Kitchen* is another book I only discovered as an adult which puts the symbolism of food at its centre and in which I find, like *Green Eggs and Ham*, strange depths.

At first *In the Night Kitchen* seems to be about a little boy called Mickey's bad dream after he is made furious by a 'racket in the night' – which some have suggested, quite convincingly, might be the noise of his parents having sex – and tumbles out of bed and out of his clothes.

What follows is a midnight feast turned horror movie, as he falls into a kitchen where the jars of jam and oats and baby syrup have morphed into the skyline of a brutal city. Three bakers (triplets who look like Oliver Hardy of 'Laurel and Hardy' in white coats, with Hitler moustaches and chef's hats) try to cook Mickey, mixing him up in their cake batter until only his flailing hand is visible, then lifting it into the oven where he begins to steam and bake. It has hints of classical tragedy, of Thyestes unknowingly being served a feast of his own sons, or nightmares of still being alive in the coffin as it incinerates. For Sendak, a Polish Jew who lost many members of his extended family in the Holocaust during what he called the 'terrible situation' of his childhood (his father found out about their fate on the day of Sendak's Bar Mitzvah), the symbolism of the oven must also have been unavoidable.

In all these books the shadow of Nazism seems unavoidable.

But then Mickey does not accept his fate – instead he sits up, ruining the cake. There seems to have been some confusion between his own name and the word milk, as they have letters in common. He declares, gleefully and defiantly: 'I'M NOT THE MILK AND THE MILK'S NOT ME! I'M MICKEY!'

Milk is at the beginning of it all. Breast milk or formula milk is everyone's first food. Slightly sweet. Slightly warm. Filling. As we get older, the same flavours find their way into so many comfort foods: Petit Filous, Babybels, ice creams, rice pudding, custard, bowls of cereal steeped in sweet milk, macaroni cheese, cream cheese bagels, stringy toasties, stuffed-crust double cheese pizzas, cream cakes, cheesecake, enormous buckets of caramel latte, *Goodnight Moon*'s bowl full of 'mush'.

At first, too, this flavour is linked to power. The psychoanalyst Donald Winnicott has spoken of how newborn babies have no conception of the outside world, only experiencing that when they are hungry they eat, so that it appears as if milk is conjured by their need – they seem to will it into existence. Growing up means having to learn that the world can frustrate and will not magically shape itself to our desires.

Maurice Sendak's *In the Night Kitchen* contains the fantasy that the child can access unlimited milk. Having told the bakers that he is not the milk, Mickey sets about getting them some, fashioning himself an aeroplane from bread dough, grabbing a measuring cup which he uses as a dashing helmet, and flying to the top of a giant milk bottle. He dives in and his dough-clothes dissolve, leaving him to swim deep into the deep milk, utterly naked. The illustrations even show his little buttocks and genitals, due to which the book has frequently been challenged or banned in the USA. (Sendak commented: 'Mickey has a penis. *Gevalt!* Who would have thought such a thing could happen to a child?') Sendak's homosexuality – he lived with his partner Eugene Glynn for fifty years until Glynn's death – is perhaps an important factor here. He is queering the picture book, allowing a boy to enjoy his body without shame. It is a delectable dream of freedom and excess.

The American poet Rita Dove has a wonderful poem called 'After Reading *Mickey in the Night Kitchen* for the Third Time Before Bed' that captures some of the reasons people might find the picture book threatening. It begins with her daughter spreading her legs 'to find her vagina', perhaps inspired by Mickey's shameless nakedness, then demanding to see her mother's and shrieking: *'We're pink!'* In the last verse we are told that every month the little girl asks about her mother's period (another taboo fluid), before ending:

> How to tell her that it's what makes us –
> black mother, cream child.
> That we're in the pink
> and the pink's in us.

Dove's poem reveals how *In the Night Kitchen* opens a space in which both children and parents can think about bodies, flesh, fluids, intimacy, nakedness.

But the milk is also importantly *not Mickey*. He has realized he is separate from his mother. That milk will not magically appear but can only be obtained if he acts in the world, with physical or imaginative work. Mickey saves the day, pouring milk into the batter. Suddenly filled with a glorious sense of self and self-pride, Mickey crows: 'Cock a Doodle Doo!' (in thick, twirly, giant red letters) before falling back safe into his bed.

I have reached the final page. It shows a radiant sun, with rays of gold and orange and lemon and biscuit and rose gold and, in the centre, Mickey smiling contentedly in his dough suit clutching a big bottle of milk. My son is clutching his own milk. 'And that's why, thanks to Mickey,' I tell him, 'we have cake every morning.'

Wait though – we have cake every morning? *Cake?* Do we? Did I just say that aloud to my child, as if stating a fact? Who has cake every morning for God's sake?

It's a brilliantly tricky last line, like a joke played on the parent. We have entered the child's world and forgotten ourselves, and now look at what we've gone and said. Sendak is always hyperaware of the parents both in the story and reading the story, their absence and presence.

Sendak is also always on the side of the child.

'Of course, we must have cake every morning,' Gruff replies, smiling up at me.

4. The Wild Rumpus

On boys and monsters

Death is represented in the picture book, almost exclusively, as a mouth with teeth.

Mickey in his pie reminds us that food and danger are all mixed up. To eat is pleasure, but to be eaten is pain. The gingerbread man runs as fast as he can but is ingested. We flee from the tiger's mouth, the wolf's mouth, the dragon's mouth, the bear's mouth. To die is to become Witch with Chips, owl ice cream, Gruffalo crumble.

Chicken Licken, Henny Penny, Cocky Locky, Ducky Lucky, Drakey Lakey and Goosey Loosey are gobbled down by Foxy Loxy. He licks his whiskers.

Why is this the only way we allow picture book characters to die? As a death, at least, to be eaten is not wasteful. It has a kind of rationale to it. And being eaten leaves – usefully for the illustrator – no corpse. It is a kind of magic trick: you are there and then gone. There is also, perhaps, the idea that being swallowed whole is somehow *reversible*, at least in the child's mind, which makes it more tolerable. Jonah squats in the belly of the whale. In Prokofiev's musical composition *Peter and the Wolf*, if we listen carefully at the end, we hear the duck still quacking inside the wolf's tummy. In one of my children's favourite books, John Fardell's *The Day Louis Got Eaten*, the Sabre-Toothed Yomper swallows the Spiny-Backed Guzzler swallows the Undersnatch swallows the Grabular swallows the Gulper who has swallowed Louis. In one picture we can see them all, like Russian dolls nesting within each other, or a vast turducken, and then – burp – they all come back up.

Or should the question be, why is this the only way we allow picture book characters to kill? It is power displayed in its simplest form, as in a game on a mobile phone – you beat the other players and accrue their energy. Your shark eats the fish or begins to flicker; life draining away. Eating is often used in picture books to elicit an uneasy laugh from shocked children, who aren't quite sure what just happened or whether they should be laughing. In *Tadpole's Promise*, by Jeanne Willis and Tony Ross, tadpole and his beautiful rainbow friend, the caterpillar, grow up and he, er, digests her. In *I Want My Hat Back* by Jon Klassen, on the very funny last page, the rabbit's disappearance is explained by bear's unconvincing denial ('I would not eat a rabbit').

Perhaps we allow these stories to depict murder in the form of eating because, well, we want to normalize the relationship between murder and eating. As a mother, of course, I'm grateful to the Normans for their euphemisms pork, beef and venison; to sausages for their facelessness. Their intensive processing is likely to be the reason sausages feature so often in children's culture – in Carle, in Kerr, in *Mr Skinny*, in *Punch and Judy*. In an interview with *The Guardian*, Allan Ahlberg observed of his oeuvre: 'I like the word flabbergasted, I like the name Horace and I seem to write quite a lot about sausages.' At one point, Allan and Janet Ahlberg even worked on the idea for a book called *Sausages!* where if a reader spotted a mistake they had to yell 'Sausages!' Perhaps it is because sausages are 'Neat and hushed', as the poet Mark Waldron has it in his marvellous poem 'The Sausage Factory', though I can never forget his final image of them: 'wee circus elephants, / gripping the tail of the one that goes before, / marching uncertainly away from death.' The famous schoolyard nonsense rhyme 'The sausage is a cunning bird' finds amusement, similarly, in zoomorphizing this least animal of meats, imagining it 'makes its nest in gravy'.

I'm aware that the knowledge of where meat comes from is trickling through, slowly, into Gruff's consciousness. And it makes me ashamed. I am waiting for unanswerable questions; for him to realize we are the wolf outside the houses of the three little pigs. I am the troll who listens for the billy goats trip-trapping over our bridge.

The bleakest story in all of children's literature is about meat. It is called 'How Some Children Played at Slaughtering' and was collected by the Brothers Grimm. Part II begins:

There was once a father who slaughtered a pig, and his children saw that. In the afternoon, when they began playing, one child said to the other, 'You be the little pig, and I'll be the butcher.' He then took a shiny knife and slit his little brother's throat.

(trans. Jack Zipes)

In this tale, what our children look upon has consequences. Violent images beget violence.

Is it dangerous, then, to read our children picture books in which characters are cruel or brutal? Child psychologist Bruno Bettelheim argued otherwise in his book *The Uses of Enchantment*, one of the great defences of disturbing fairy tales. He claimed that in modern life:

> There is a widespread refusal to let children know that the source of much that goes wrong in life is due to our own natures . . . But children know that they are not always good; and often, even when they are, they would prefer not to be. This contradicts what they are told by their parents, and therefore makes the child a monster in his own eyes.

In contemporary society, where children are constantly exposed to the capitalist mantra that they must be 'true to themselves', this contradiction has only got worse. Actual adult life is a constant process of denying your own desires – forcing yourself to shun the lie-in, the sugar, the burger, the wine, the affair, the impulse to tell the boss what you think. Forcing yourself to mop up the vomit, work late, make the phone call, bake the birthday cake. Yet we often fail to teach our children that 'good' is not something we are but something we do. That 'good', anyway, is mainly used by parents as a synonym for 'obedient', even though that is not the same thing at all. Obedience is not a virtue. We say 'What a good girl' to the child who we have made share her sweets, although we know inside she is shuddering with resentment. 'Follow your dreams!' we declare, although we know children dream (as we do) of being 'bad'.

If we follow Bettelheim's logic, there is an important function, then, to children's poems, tales and books that acknowledge the existence of monsters: as enemies, as friends, as doubles. They make appearances from the earliest children's nursery rhymes, as in the German poem 'Das bucklige Männlein':

> When I go to my small room,
> To eat stewed fruit
> A humpy little man is there
> Gobbling it.

The humpy little man is the self's dark twin, sabotaging everything: disfigured, grumpy, devouring.

To return to Maurice Sendak, he is of course most famous for his own rendering of the beasts of self in *Where the Wild Things Are* (1963), which has sold over 20 million copies. The book seems to have been formed from memories of the gulf between desire and duty. In an interview with *The Jewish Chronicle* he recalled how often, when dinner was on the table and his mother had been calling him repeatedly, she'd make him feel guilty by saying: 'Your cousins, you know they're your age. They don't play ball. They're dead. They're in a concentration camp . . . and you don't come up and eat.'

The book was originally going to be called *Where the Wild Horses Are*. Sendak's editor, Ursula Nordstrom, liked this poetic title, but then Sendak realized he couldn't draw horses. After he told her it wasn't working, she said, 'Maurice, what *can* you draw?'

'Vilder chaiah' was something his mother would call him, the Yiddish version of 'wild thing'. In the end, inspired by a shiva after someone in the family had died, he decided to base the 'wild things' on his older relatives from Europe: 'They were unkempt. Their teeth were horrifying. They had hair unravelling out of their noses. And they'd pick you up and hug you and kiss you. "Aggghh. Oh, we could eat you up," they'd say. And we knew they would eat anything. Anything.' His very act of drawing them as grotesque, humpy creatures could be seen as a kind of cruelty. The book itself is an aggressive act by a bad little boy, wanting to wound.

This subversiveness has always discomforted parents, many of whom claimed at the time that the book was too scary. (Sendak suggested they should 'go to hell', while if children couldn't handle the story, they should 'go home' or 'wet your pants. Do whatever you like.') One of the most amusing anecdotes about the book is Sendak's recollection of a fight with his safety-conscious publisher, who wanted to change the dinner from 'hot' to 'warm' at the end of the book. 'It was going to burn the kid,' Sendak recalled. 'I couldn't believe it. But it turned into a real world war . . . Just trying to convey how dopey "warm" sounded. Unemotional. Undramatic. Everything about that book is "hot".' *Where the Wild Things Are* is a dangerous book, but the hot dinner is perhaps the least dangerous thing in it.

For me, the subversiveness lies in the fact that it is a book about power. Although many commentators, and Sendak himself, have spoken of it as a book about rage, I find Max disturbing because he doesn't look angry – or at least not in the incontinent, temper-tantrum way I associate with small children. This boy has chosen to put on his wolf suit, then deliberately constructs some kind of grim lair, where a tortured teddy bear dangles like a warning. Tailed and with his fork aloft, he leaps towards his dog, smiling as purposefully as a devil. His declaration 'I'LL EAT YOU UP!' is not the impotent cry of infant rage, but a threat. He wants to possess the mother utterly; to own her by subduing her will and making her silent. ('For each man kills the thing he loves,' as Oscar Wilde noted.) As the forest grows in Max's room, he doesn't look furious so much as smug, then giddy with delight.

In the land of the Wild Things too, Max does not act out his rage, but lives out his fantasy of total control. Sendak's father once told him when he was ill that if he could look out of the window without blinking he would see an angel (naturally, Sendak did). Max also gains uncanny power by not blinking once. Here he can tame and intimidate everyone. As King, he is treated with respect. The Wild Things bow. He can be as loud and silly as he wishes (in a bold move, when Mickey participates in the wild rumpus there are three whole wordless spreads, allowing the child to supply their own rumpus, although as an adult reader I always find the silence uncomfortable, chicken out, and choose to fill it with whoopings that fall dolefully flat). Max can punish his subjects, too, on a dictator's arbitrary whim, sending them to bed without any supper.

Essentially, then, he gains adult freedoms but also adult responsibilities, and finds that ruling over others is not always pleasurable. Being in charge is lonely. He realizes he wants to be where he is loved 'best of all'. Although this might suggest he learns some empathy with his mother, the illustrations undermine this reading – this is a picture book about the relationship between a mother and son in which the mother is never actually seen. Her reality is not important. The book is about Max resigning himself to his position as a child.

And what about that last, famous page, which boldly has no picture? The mother, I would argue, has lost her nerve. Despite all Max's misbehaviour, she cannot bring herself to let him go hungry. Max doesn't have to say sorry. He has discovered he does have power after all; the enormous power that comes from being loved. A picture of him eating the hot supper would be an irrelevance – it is the *feeling* that is important. How it makes Max glow inside.

It is a comforting story for children because it tells the truth that even if you behave badly, your mother still probably loves you unconditionally. This, understandably, is not a truth many adults want children to grasp.

My son likes to think of himself as good. A Goody not a Baddy. In the games he pesters me to play on the school run he is a sauropod and I am the theropod. He is Scooby-Doo ('Yoinks!') and I am 'The Dark Mummy'. He is Chewbacca and I am an AT-AT walker firing at him: *pew pew*. On some very long walks to Morrisons, being a boy can strike me as gruelling – a never-ending chase scene. Is anything marketed to boys that doesn't involve fighting? Life is figured as a perpetual battle in which you have to be good or you're bad; you have to be best or you're dead. As in that chant which has endured virtually unchanged since Roman times, if you're not the king of the castle you're a dirty rascal by default. (The poet Horace wrote down the Latin verse for the game in 20 BC: 'Rex erit qui recte faciet; / Qui non faciet, non erit.')

One of the ways in which Gruff manages to keep a sense of his own goodness is via Oneie (like 'Onesie' without the 's'), his bad hand. His other hand is called Double Trouble but is actually much better behaved. Oneie first appeared when we were shopping in a Tesco Metro and Gruff took a blueberry from a packet in the fruit aisle. I told him if we hadn't paid for it, it was stealing and he could get in big trouble. 'Oneie did it,' he replied. Oneie has since been blamed for running his finger along filthy fences, all breakages and spillages, the unspooling of entire toilet rolls, the repeated tipping over of Gruff's toybox, and a similar incident with Pick 'n' Mix. ('Oneie thought little children were supposed to have nice sweets,' Gruff explained.) Occasionally I have heard Gruff talking to him. Oneie, it should be said, is not uncomplicated. He often wilts with remorse; curls into a lonesome fist.

Perhaps the only picture book to equal Sendak's as a portrait of the monstrous self is David McKee's *Not Now, Bernard* (1980).

McKee is more famous for Elmer, the rainbow-coloured patchwork elephant who, amongst other things, decorates a plastic dinner set in my kitchen. Every evening, after the carnage of mealtime, I wipe my children's hands, sweep the crumbs, rinse the bib, scrape baked beans off Elmer into the bin and recall the story of his invention. McKee was walking down the street in Devon with his wife, Violet, and daughter, Chantel, when a boy said, 'Look, there's a nigger.' McKee's wife was Anglo-Indian. McKee realized the boy was talking about his beautiful daughter. Elmer became a story about celebrating your true colours.

McKee is a moralist, then, but he is an unpredictable one. His books are fabular, yet, unlike that first Elmer, later ones often deliver confusing messages. His Melric series seems to advocate unshakable loyalty to their king, even when he is mistaken. His book *Denver*, about a rich philanthropist who makes the error of sharing out his money equally, has been savaged by Polly Toynbee as 'Ayn Rand for baby beginners, trickle-down economics for trustafarian toddlers, a nursery Hayek for every little Conservative'.

Not Now, Bernard is his simplest but most ambiguous tale. The drawings of Bernard's house, with its intricate seventies rugs and lampshades and TV dinner (sausages of course, always sausages) are stunning in their lurid, off-kilter realism. It is about a child whose parents ignore him. They are always busy doing something more important than attending to their son – hammering, getting something from a cupboard, watering a houseplant – and his attempts to engage them with a simple hello are met with 'Not now, Bernard'. The parents are always drawn with their backs to Bernard. When the mother speaks to him her eyes are always closed. When Bernard mentions there is a monster in the garden that is going to eat him, this reaction does not change. The monster eats him. The monster comes into the house, roars, bites the father, breaks the toys, etc. The parents still don't notice. 'Not now, Bernard' they say.

Is the monster Bernard? Francis Spufford has noted, in *The Child that Books Built*, that the monster is 'very much Bernard-shaped and Bernard-sized'. Michael Rosen has called it a 'cautionary tale', suggesting that neglecting your children may turn them into monsters. In this metaphor, then, does Bernard genuinely become monstrous? Or just fantasize about being a monster? On one wall is a picture that, if you squint carefully, seems to show a man with a gun holding up a petrol station – people fleeing; a woman with her hands up. It seems as though it might foretell Bernard's destiny. Heartbreakingly, the monster ends this story in bed with his teddy, saying: 'But I'm a monster.'

Just as Max discovered, monstrousness changes nothing – but Max is still loved. Bernard is still unloved.

There is another way to read it too, though, in which Bernard does get eaten. 'Hello, monster,' Bernard says, smiling at the monster, and the monster meets his eye.

In her 'Stroppy Author' blog, children's writer Anne Rooney has noted: 'He knows the monster is going to eat him and he *still* goes to say hello to it – because even bad attention is better than no attention.' A fellow reader, Rooney notes, called it 'a book about suicide for kids'. Neglect might lead our children towards bad decisions, bad people, a quick and cruel end.

Coming back from the train station in Peckham at dusk last night, in cold violet air, frozen fish fingers swinging in a plastic bag by my leg, I passed two teenage boys. They were near the high school gates, beside a few brave daffodils trying to burn through a crust of snow. A younger boy approached in his hoodie. 'About time, yeah,' I overheard one of the teenagers say. 'I was gonna have to stab you.'

I walked on, head down. Averting my eyes like Bernard's mother. Wondering what had led that boy in the hoodie to walk out of his home and towards his monster. It is hard for me to imagine what it is like right now to be a young man growing up in South London, where gangs and knives are a fact of life. I try not to think about what it might be like for Gruff in a few years.

My own childhood was so sheltered by comparison. I think the first time I realized that cruelty existed in the real world, and not just in storybooks, wasn't until I was in reception. It must have been spring. At half-three, Dad let me run to the playing field, down a steep slope behind the school. All day there had been whispers about a plague of thousands of frogs; a weird exodus. In my recollection the grass is pinging with them, although can that be true? Small bodies with damp, crooked legs; chests pale, pulsing fungi. We tried to catch the spill of them in cupped hands. They were so cute, like tiny wind-up toys.

On the barbed-wire fence at the back another child showed me a row of spiked frogs, like a medieval warning. Cold, congealed flesh. She was breathless with thrilled indignation. Big boys did it, she said, as if their masculinity was the explanation.

*

In *Angry Arthur* (1982), written by Hiawyn Oram and illustrated by Satoshi Kitamura, there is, more clearly than in *Not Now, Bernard*, no monster but the boy himself. Tortured by fury, he helplessly flails in the mess of a rage which expands page by page until it destroys the galaxy. And for what? Because he is not allowed to stay up to watch a western on TV. Goodies and Baddies, then. The TV is depicted by Kitamura with smoke and arrows pouring out of it into the living room, battles spilling into the domestic space. *Angry Arthur* is perhaps one of the first picture books to deal with our fear of toddlers becoming addicted to screens; our sense that televisual violence might seep into the real world to brainwash our children.

Except it is not just the lack of TV but the lack of power that makes Arthur angry. When the mother comes in to tell him to switch it off, her shadow looms large and menacing. She has disrupted the male fantasy. He sees the walls of his cell, his chains, and cannot endure her authority over him. In a stunning series of images, Arthur's limitless fury smashes his home, his street, his town, the earth (which cracks like an eggshell), and eventually the entire universe in a 'universe quake' that seems to break the conventions of the picture book itself, despite his family impotently telling him 'that's enough'.

Kitamura has since illustrated a great many titles (I would highly recommend his collaborations with the poet John Agard), but this masterpiece was, astonishingly, his first book. Born in Tokyo in 1956, he had no formal art training, but had spent his childhood fascinated by forms of art – like many Japanese children he often drew on the pavement and roads; at school he drew caricatures of teachers; he pored over comics; he delighted in Kamishibai shows, a popular street entertainment until television took over, where the Kamishibai man would cycle up, sell children cheap sweets as an admission fee, then from a box on his bike take out a series of hand-painted sliding pictures to tell a tale.

Having decided to be an illustrator, Kitamura tried twenty publishers before he met Klaus Flugge of Andersen Press, who asked him to illustrate *Angry Arthur*. It was by a South African writer, Hiawyn Oram, who recalled growing up under apartheid – its unfairness; its carelessness with human lives. She had been an advertising copywriter, writing ads for toothpaste, chocolate bars and Lucozade before her first children's book, *Skittlewonder and the Wizard* (1980). A week later, Kitamura had produced a complete, perfect set of roughs.

Editor and writer Max Porter, author of *Grief is the Thing with Feathers*, has named as his 'favourite page of any book' the one on which Arthur creates a 'universe quake' that seems to destroy everything (except multiple vibrating Arthurs), saying: 'For me it is right up there with Ted Hughes' Crow, Francis Bacon's Popes or Mahler's Ninth.' Porter also notes that, in 1982, it was easy to read it as a book about a nuclear weapon. 'This is the boy pressing the red button, becoming destroyer of worlds.'

In the end Arthur is alone, in his bed on a tiny chunk of Mars, unable – despite thinking and thinking – to remember what triggered his anger. 'He never did remember,' the text tells us. 'Can you?' In a way this is a useful conclusion.

It seems to ask not only whether we recall what caused Arthur's fury, but what causes our own rages. It speaks to the listening children with their meltdowns over spoons; the reading parents, with their snapping impatience over spilt juice. The whole book is about perspective – how do we let little things become so grotesquely outsized? Arthur goes to sleep and, we might presume, wakes up with the universe restored to its correct proportions.

But what if it can't be restored? The only cure for anger that the book seems to offer is the passage of time, but there are many men who seem unable to grow out of raging against their own impotence. What if Arthur is on Reddit now, still mesmerized by screens, typing furiously about cucks and feminazis? What if thoughtless, aggrieved men will annihilate humanity, and no one survive but a few friends of Elon Musk on Mars?

Everything might end like this, *nothing more than bits in space*.

Boys, though.

It's always boys in the newspapers stabbing each other; misunderstanding consent. It's always boys playing with monsters in these books. Boys filled with rage. Boys fighting. Boys roaring. HULK SMASH.

Or, that is, it's always boys we depict like this. These are the stories we tell about boys to our boys. It's not *Angry Anna* or *Not Now, Bertha*. Peter Rabbit misbehaves while his sisters Flopsy, Mopsy and Cotton-tail are 'good little bunnies'. In Elfrida Vipont and Raymond Briggs' *The Elephant and the Bad Baby*, in which the title characters are a kind of two-year-old's Bonnie and Clyde, stealing lollipops, pies and buns and going 'rumpeta, rumpeta, rumpeta', with the shopkeepers chasing after them, the elephant and eventually Bad Baby are both revealed to be boys ('He never *once* said please!'). In many of these tales too, whilst there is some notional punishment, it is the wild pleasure of the mischief that is memorable – the thrill of destruction, the illicit cake, the chase. What if these stories do, after all, have a negative effect on boys, naughtiness begetting naughtiness?

Girls are sugar and spice, it is only boys who are 'frogs and snails and puppy-dog's tails'. The first time I read Gruff that rhyme I saw him crumple. 'What did you just say?' he asked, his voice wavery with tears. 'That's not nice.'

No one seems to defend boy's culture any more, but growing up there was much I liked about it: adventure, courage, jokes. I had no interest in pinkness, pony hair, dolls that wept actual tears, or any of the other sorry trivialities with which I was apparently supposed to distract myself. Because my dad only had daughters, he instilled in us a love of *The Beano*, Flash Gordon and James Bond. He loved watching Goodies beat Baddies, then rewinding and watching it again. He would show us clips of Bruce Lee fights over and over on the video, until I identified with that stray kitten perpetually watching the struggle in the Colosseum. Jason fought the Harryhausen skeletons, then the bones sprang back to life. Rocky Balboa chased chickens in infinite circles.

I wanted to be as cool as Indiana Jones or Dr Peter Venkman, or at least Garfield the cat, decorating my room with examples of his withering sarcasm. *I think I'm allergic to mornings!* (Unfortunately my wit was not quite as sharp. At four, when told to wish one of my sister's little friends Happy New Year, I managed only: 'Happy New Dirt, Ruthie Rat.')

I didn't want to *be* male, you understand. I wanted to be the one cool girl who got to hang out with the boys. I wanted to be Sigourney Weaver in *Ghostbusters*, Marion Ravenwood drinking men under the table in *Raiders of the Lost Ark*, Princess Leia leading the rebels. In reception I was proud to be friends with Chris and Matthew, who taught me to do Chinese burns. I remember going to Matthew's house for tea and having a mixture of canned French onion and oxtail soup, the darkest tasting thing I could imagine, and him teaching me the word *bitch*. On Valentine's Day I sent a card to Simon Hickey saying: 'Be my Valentine or I'll do Karate on you.'

Best Friends for Frances by Russell and Lillian Hoban was my introduction to feminism. I was outraged when Frances's best friend, Albert, wouldn't let her join in his 'wander' as he planned to do things he thought she couldn't do. Frances asks him what those things might be:

'Catching snakes,' said Albert. 'Throwing stones at telephone poles. A little frog work maybe. Walking on fences. Whistling with grass blades. Looking for crow feathers.'

In irritation, Frances takes her little sister Gloria out on a rival wander with a picnic hamper, sacks and eggs for games, a jar of frogs, balloons and lollies, and a sign saying:

BEST FRIENDS
OUTING
NO BOYS

I recreated this protest. A photograph still exists. I am crunching an apple with my funny little sister and small friends, our tops off in the sunshine against a backdrop of rosebay willowherb, holding our first placard.

*

Were there boys' books then? I mean, I guess there were. I guess they just used to call them books. In the forty-two books Dr Seuss wrote, not one has a female lead in its central story. But I don't remember many picture books that seemed aimed exclusively at an audience of boys. Some of Richard Scarry's perhaps, like *Cars and Trucks and Things That Go* (1974), in their ridiculously detailed, exhaustive drawings of vehicles ('gravel truck', 'asphalt oil spreader', 'asphalt dumpcart', 'asphalt finisher'), but these did feature Officer Flossy in hot pursuit and Mistress Mouse doing the repairs (and Ma puts on the snow chains).

It only seems to be in recent years that manufacturers have realized dividing up any product by gender is a way of making money, as parents of a son and daughter feel pressured to buy everything twice. It was also only in the 1970s that the idea that boys were failing to engage with reading began to gain traction. In the USA the National Assessment of Educational Progress (NAEP) began undertaking reading assessments in 1971, and girls have outscored boys every year since. Over the decades, one of the 'solutions' that has grown in popularity is to pitch books specifically at little boys (even though you could have argued they were the default audience beforehand). It begins with the assumption that boys must be struggling because they think reading is boring and 'girly'. To raise their literacy, books need to be made subversive and macho.

What do these boys' books consist of? Soldiers and cowboys – those variations on violence which, I suppose, were the classic male genres – are no longer generally considered acceptable (even in my childhood I can't recall seeing them, though grown-ups still occasionally spoke of 'Red Indians'). Instead the violence is now situated in a fantasy or securely historical world: monsters, pirates, aliens, knights, zombies, robots, T-Rexes, anything 'spooky'. All the characters in this world will, in defiance of biological reality, be male. Boyhood, these books say, is about fighting and bravely laughing off danger. As neuroscientist Cordelia Fine has noted in her book *Delusions of Gender*, priming subjects to be aware of their gender before a task – for example, reminding a girl that she is a girl before doing a maths task – can actually have a huge impact on results. Members of a group who know there are negative stereotypes about them can become anxious about their performance, with their ability to perform therefore hindered, a phenomenon Fine refers to as 'stereotype threat'. It might be argued that boys' books are counterproductive, reminding boys that they are boys and therefore supposed to find books dull, even as the texts attempt so sycophantically to titillate their supposedly jaded palates.

Also, noticeably and increasingly, these 'boy' books are full of yukky stuff: snot, farts, burps, underpants, bottoms, toilets, sick. Interestingly, it is the bodily waste products that French theorist Julia Kristeva associates with abjection and disgust that leak through many of these pages. It is worth observing that Kristeva has linked our taboos around these substances, which are both part of us and yet must be ejected, to the fundamental rejection of the maternal body. At the time young boys are trying to become independent of their mothers, we might ask why they are seen to relish the excremental so much.

Not that the writers have usually thought very deeply about this. The bulk of these titles are a lazy, focus-grouped mashup of the same elements: *The Burp that Saved the World. No-Bot, the Robot with no Bottom. Robo-Snot. The Dinosaur that Pooped a Planet* (I was actually shocked, I have to say, by the sheer quantity of loose yellow diarrhoea in this one). *Monsters Love Underpants. Pirates Love Underpants. Aliens Love Dinopants.* The last three are part of the enormously successful Underpants franchise by author Claire Freedman and illustrator Ben Cort. Freedman's website tells us the genesis story – apparently, after ten years of writing: 'A spaceship landed in her neighbour's back garden and some funny aliens stepped out. Then – would you believe it – they stole the red spotted bloomers hanging on their washing line! Of course she had to write about it – and *Aliens Love Underpants* was born!' To which I can only say that no, I wouldn't believe it. 'Red spotted bloomers' is the kind of wholly unconvincing detail that makes me question the veracity of the whole pants-mad aliens metanarrative.

I've never been fond of toilet humour, so I suppose this isn't the sort of male culture I would have enjoyed as a child myself. In fact, I'm sure we would never have been allowed a book with the word 'Poo' in the title in the house. An obsession with cleanliness was one of the factors that darkened my father's miserable childhood. He was constantly fed syrup of figs to clean him out; circumcised when he was four (an event he never forgave his parents for) because it was more 'hygienic'. Granny Pollard thought breastfeeding was a dirty habit. In her chilly house, the toilet roll was hidden under a dolly's frilly skirts.

'Loo' was forbidden for being common. A poo was called a 'mess'. After we 'had a mess' we were encouraged to spray a smog of floral air freshener.

As a mother of a son, too, I find these books ugly. Not that I'm squeamish, not now. I've re-educated my gag reflex. Your sense of taboo really does loosen after you've found yourself shitting during childbirth; watched that entire slick organ, the placenta, lug out of your body. Babies are tiny animals constantly sitting in their own piss and dung, letting off rich scents, yet they are somehow the opposite of revolting. As a mother you watch the loose explosions of yellow slowly thicken and darken. You fish faeces like polished brown stones out of the bath. You wake in the middle of the night and shower clumps of puke, its bile-and-nana stink, from rainbow jimjams. You pick your own daughter's nose.

But *milk and stories* is our special time, cosied up on the bed. I want to teach Gruff about the lovely, intricate world and all its enchantments. I want us to fall under a magic spell, not a farty smell.

The first couple of globally successful 'poo' books should probably not be blamed. They were both, rarely for picture books in the UK, translations – *Everybody Poos* (1977) by Taro Gomi, from the Japanese, and *The Story of the Little Mole Who Knew it Was None of His Business* (1989) by Werner Holzwarth and Wolf Erlbruch, from the German. Both have quite a charming, matter-of-factness in their acknowledgement of our status as animals, and are probably useful tools around the period of potty training. Taro Gomi's *Everybody Poos*, particularly, isn't cheap at all. He has said in an interview with the *Japan Foundation Newsletter* that the book was inspired by a trip to a zoo one winter morning to interview a vet:

> I got there before it opened, so most of the cages weren't cleaned yet. There was a lot of poop around. It was a cold winter morning, and steam was coming out from each pile as the morning sunshine streamed down on it. It was such a vivid scene.

I love that warm, painterly image, and it is notable he finds a strange beauty in his illustrations too – the golden loaf of elephant's poo, the mouse's tiny grains, the fish's delicate stick, the bird's pale splutter, the pangolin's modest burial.

Although his publishers argued over it, children immediately responded to his honesty about this weird substance that comes from their bodies. Gomi notes: 'It was a funny, curious, and interesting thing for them. One boy who loved the book sent me cards entitled "Today's Poop" almost every day for six months.'

Potty-training books are now commonplace – showing, as Gomi did, the ritual of wipe and flush. Unfortunately, books which just shout POOPYPANTS and then wait expectantly for hilarity to ensue are commonplace too. (I am sad to report the children usually oblige.)

*

Wait, though – while yukky jokes have only recently been sanctioned by the gatekeepers of children's literature (adults), let's not pretend that small children have not enjoyed them forever. It's just that previously they spread orally, in whispers and giggles, from child to child, rather than from commercially benefitting grown-ups. 'The one who smelt it dealt it.' Or:

> Tell Tale tit
> Your tongue shall be slit,
> And all the dogs in the town
> Shall have a little bit.

Or:

> Scab and matter custard,
> Green snot pies,
> Dead dog's giblets,
> Dead cat's eyes,
> And a cup of sick to wash it down.

Versions of all of these circulated in my playground. I came across them again recently in the married couple Iona and Peter Opie's masterful piece of research, the anthology *The Lore and Language of Schoolchildren* (1959). Although not picture book writers or illustrators, as chroniclers of all the children's culture that *isn't* written down or illustrated, the Opies had a huge impact on the genre.

Exiled by the London Blitz to Bedfordshire, the couple's obsession with rituals and rhymes began when they were walking by a cornfield and Iona was pregnant. One of them lifted a red-and-black spotted bug on to their finger ('I forget whose finger it was,' Iona Opie said. 'Somebody's finger') and chanted:

> Ladybird, ladybird,
> Fly away home.
> Your house is on fire
> And your children all gone;
> All except one
> And that's little Ann,
> And she has crept under
> The warming pan.

As the ladybird took off, they found themselves wondering what the words meant and who had written them. They decided to find out, though it was not easy for the Opies to launch themselves into such a substantial project, given they had no academic background or qualifications. Soon they had established a working pattern where Peter did the writing, while Iona did the research (he nicknamed her 'old mother shuffle paper'). For a long time they were so poor they famously picked nettles from the park for vegetables at dinner. They were fortunate that a librarian at the Bodleian in Oxford found them collecting riddles, so recommended them to the Oxford University Press.

The Lore and Language of Schoolchildren is a book that influenced a whole generation of picture book writers. It references, for example, the trope of *the tale without end*, a 'stock joke' that usually begins: 'It was a dark and stormy night, the rain came down in torrents, there were brigands on the mountains, and thieves, and the chief said unto Antonio: "Antonio, tell us a story".' This is almost verbatim how Janet and Allan Ahlberg's *It Was a Dark and Stormy Night* begins, except in their book there are also wolves for good measure. Just a couple of pages later, the Opies refer to the multiplications of the word 'dark' in spooky kids' tales meant to frighten others by torchlight:

> In a dark, dark wood, there was a dark, dark house,
> And in that dark, dark house, there was a dark, dark
> room . . .

Instantly, we can see where the Ahlbergs' *Funnybones*, which tells the adventures of big skeleton and little skeleton, sprang from too. ('On a dark dark hill / there was a dark dark town . . .') *The Lore and Language of Schoolchildren* must have been very well thumbed in the Ahlberg house.

Janet and Allan Ahlberg specialize in likeable monsters. Their oeuvre is full of them: cheerful ghosts playing football; a giant with a smiling baby on his knee; Wolf reading a story to the three little pigs with glasses perched on his snout, and of course, everyone's favourite warm-hearted criminal Burglar Bill. A husband and wife team like the Opies, Janet and Allan married when they were both students at Sunderland College. After trying various jobs (postman, plumber, gravedigger) Allan became a primary school teacher. Janet started illustrating non-fiction craft books of the type that involved empty yoghurt pots. It was only when Allan was in his late thirties that Janet asked him to write a story for her to illustrate, for a change. Allan Ahlberg has said it was like 'a key turning in my back'.

Although they sometimes worked with other creative partners, arguably their finest work was undertaken together in the 37 picture books they created over the next 20 years, seeing themselves as book 'makers' who oversaw every aspect of design. Many of their books have an interactive element that makes them almost like a game parent and child can play together – pulling tiny letters from envelopes in *The Jolly Postman*, peeping through the holes in *Peepo!*, playing I-Spy in *Each Peach Pear Plum*. Often they combine traditional sources (nursery rhymes, fairy tales) with a particular twentieth-century charm – the witch in *The Jolly Postman* lives in a 'gingerbread bungalow' and receives a mail-order catalogue from Hobgoblin Supplies Ltd selling non-stick cauldrons and 'Little Boy Pie Mix', reminiscent of the Avon and Littlewoods catalogues that everyone on our estate had delivered. For me they seem like time capsules, capturing childhood in the 1970s and 1980s.

Allan Ahlberg said that: 'Just because a book is tiny and its readers are little doesn't mean it can't be perfect. On its own scale, it can be as good as Tolstoy or Jane Austen.' The books he created with Janet Ahlberg fulfilled this promise, until her painfully early death from breast cancer in 1994, aged fifty.

Allan was born illegitimate in 1940s Croydon. Adopted, he grew up poor in Oldbury in the Black Country, a place that smelt of its local plastic and glue factories. His new mum was a cleaner, his dad a labourer. In his earliest years, the occasional bomb would fall. His mum would make up a den for him under the kitchen table with his toast and soft toys, and in his lovely memoir *The Bucket: Memories of an Inattentive Childhood*, Ahlberg vividly recalls 'that little secret place with its green tablecloth hanging down, velvet tassels and a fringe'. He has said that the *Peepo!* baby, with its tin bath, was him. It was a childhood of clips round the ear, Tizer, model soldiers, few books.

His story makes me think of my own father's. He was born in Salford, a city with smog so thick that sometimes you bumped into lamp posts. A city of chimneys and factory gates. When he was born, they couldn't afford a cot so he slept in a cupboard drawer, like the baby in *Burglar Bill*.

Both Ahlberg and my father remembered being caned at school. Ahlberg has described how, 'If you were sent to the headmaster, he would take out a bamboo cane with one end burnt black to harden it, and bring it down on the tips of your fingers.' But Ahlberg got into grammar school, as did my dad.

Once there, my dad remembered poring over novels about angry young men: *Billy Liar*; *Alfie*; *Room at the Top*. Realizing the future his father had mapped out wasn't the only one, he decided, he often said, 'to change his script'. For a bright, working-class boy there were still ways you could alter the narrative of your life.

*

Burglar Bill (1977) was my favourite of the Ahlbergs' perfect books as a child. It deals with masculinity and misbehaviour (and includes poo), but is also full of love and marvels. In 'John Wayne and Sibelius *or* The Train Has Rain in It', The Philippa Pearce Lecture he delivered in 2016, Ahlberg describes how *Burglar Bill* came to life when he was teaching a reception class in the 1970s, the register with the children's addresses in it open in front of him:

And off we'd go . . . Burglar Bill walks down Severn Road until he comes to number . . . hm – quick glance at register . . . number 8 where Alice Hicks lives. Meanwhile Alice Hicks snaps to attention and looks rather pleased with herself. Burglar Bill creeps into the hall – that's a nice umbrella, says Burglar Bill – I'll have that, and he puts it into his sack. Burglar Bill creeps into the living room – that's a nice antique clock, says Burglar Bill. I'll have that, and he puts it into his sack. Burglar Bill creeps into the kitchen. Here Alice Hicks' mummy is making a nice cheese and pickle sandwich for Alice to eat when she comes home from school. That's a nice . . . MUMMY, says Burglar Bill, I'll have her, and he puts her into his sack. Thereafter, the possibilities of the story, whatever they might have been, collapse. The children – all of them – completely absorbed in the possibility that Burglar Bill would come to their house and put their mummy in a sack – sit up rigidly on the story mat – like little tethered self-important balloons tapping themselves on the chest, some of them, hoping to get the nod.

It's interesting to see how Bill's catchphrase 'I'll have that' was one of the first things to develop. Burglar Bill makes children see that one of our earliest, most basic impulses – to want to possess things, to cry 'MINE!' – has consequences for other people. It affects real lives, real homes (*their* lives! *Their* homes!!). They feel the raw injustice as a shock.

Bill's outfit makes him a stock figure – the striped jumper, the flat cap, the black eye mask. It's now so associated with Burglar Bill that whenever a thief wears stripes or a flat cap, the newspapers love to run stories with headlines like *The Mirror*'s 'Silly Billy: Thief caught on CCTV raiding supermarket dressed as cartoon villain Burglar Bill'. ('CCTV cameras caught the crook, who bears a striking resemblance to children's storybook character Burglar Bill, breaking into a Waitrose store in Essex . . .') It's actually an outfit with a long history, though. The domino mask descends from Venetian carnival, and the trickster character of the harlequin. The striped shirt comes from the duotone uniforms of prison inmates in the 1800s, designed to make them instantly recognizable if they tried to escape. The flat cap is, of course, a marker of class. Even the name 'Bill' is familiar – there was a nineteenth-century poem published in *Punch* called 'Burglar Bill' by F. Anstey, in which the robber encounters 'Baby Bella' during a break-in and has his heart melted ('Fast he speeds across the housetops! / But his bosom throbs with bliss, / For upon his rough lips linger / Traces of a baby's kiss.')

An important thing about the book is how, like Anstey,

the Ahlbergs take their stock villain and humanize him. The terrifying image of a mother abducted in a sack, with which Allan Ahlberg originally alarmed his students, is softened. Instead a baby is (accidentally) taken in a big box that is reassuringly punctured with holes. Once Burglar Bill realizes he has stolen a baby, he is also instantly concerned with nappies and warming up bottles. The danger is domesticated. The Ahlbergs do this a lot, taking frightening figures and making them comfortingly ordinary – the fairy-tale witch has to put on her reading glasses and hangs her bat up to dry on a plastic clothes-maiden; *The Ghost Train* has a luggage rack. In a way *Burglar Bill* is a story about adults – their wicked power; their shadowy night-time lives when the children are asleep. It's also a story that reassures the child that adults are changed by parenthood: being a father means choosing to live an 'honest life'. (Although Betty, it should be said, is one of the worst mothers in all of fiction before she gets round to experiencing her epiphany. She has *lost her baby* after leaving him outside during a burglary, but when we meet her, she is still happily stealing a date and walnut cake 'with buttercream filling and icing on top' from Bill's breadbin.)

It's a very funny story. The fact that the first thing Bill steals is a toothbrush always makes me smile. Then there's the picture of the baby covered in beans. The way the baby shouts 'Again!' when Bill falls off the piano stool and bangs his nose. The first word the child says is 'Boglaboll'. The details in Janet's illustrations are absolutely delightful too – the way the cat's stripes mirror those on Bill's jumper; the House of Lords jug he uses as a teapot.

In the first draft, Allan Ahlberg has said that Bill was 'less inclined to remorse', just retiring happily to a farm at the end. Yet it is the section where Bill and Betty return stolen goods that is the most memorable – back goes the toothbrush, the goldfish, the chamber pot to the HMS *Eagle*. It is absurd and lovely. The published version ends with 'Bakery Bill' getting married, the nuclear family listening to the town hall clock strike four and passing the police station on their way home to tea, the systems of patriarchy and authority reaffirmed. In some ways it's very conservative, but it's also a quietly generous vision in that there is no punishment, only a putting right. It says that good people make bad choices, especially when they are poor. It doesn't make them monsters. Given a bit of love, they can make better choices.

It is a story that is not told often enough in our newspapers, with their cartoon headlines about Goodies and Baddies; to the boys on our street corner with their knives.

Comedies, since Aristotle, have always ended like this, with a rise in fortune for our sympathetic hero: with redemption, marriage and love. Most picture books tend towards comedy.

But the final book in this chapter is, instead, a tragedy, perhaps the great tragedy of the picture book genre: *The Lorax* (1971) by Dr Seuss. *The Lorax* is a book of nonsense verse that rings chillingly true in its depiction of environmental destruction. It begins at the end of the story, in a wasteland where the wind has a 'slow-and-sour' smell, and where 'you' might find the old Once-ler (who sounds a bit like my son's friend Oneie, now I come to think of it), lurking in his Lerkim, with teeth that sound 'grey'. The Once-ler proceeds to tell the story of how he arrived in the landscape when it was pristine, and noticed that the sour-candy-coloured Truffula Trees had the fragrance of 'fresh butterfly milk'. (What a remarkable image that is – full of innocence yet profoundly disturbing – giving him the air of a serial killer.) The Once-ler set up a business chopping down the trees to make completely amorphous, unnecessary things called Thneeds. Proud of his position as provider, he gave all of his family jobs, then set about remorselessly 'biggering / and BIGGERING' his factory until the final tree fell.

The boldness is in how Seuss lets the bad-guy tell the story – like Nabokov's Humbert Humbert in *Lolita*, the Once-ler condemns himself in his own words even as he mounts a defence. We also, strikingly, never see him, except for a pair of gloved green hands that chop trees, count coins, make calls: it is not his visage that makes him monstrous, but his actions with those ironically green fingers (an effect, incidentally, utterly destroyed in the film where the Once-ler is depicted as an ordinary-looking young man). As the child listening blurs into the 'you' being addressed, so the adult reader in some way *becomes* the Once-ler.

Though the Once-ler has success, his ambition is his

downfall. In his tragic hubris, his over-reaching, he transgresses nature. He is a kind of Midas figure whose hunger for a more prosperous future turns everything around him into past. At his touch, *now* becomes *once*; Eden is lost. 'Adults,' Seuss wrote, 'is a word that means obsolete children,' and the Once-ler embodies this obsolescence. He is not an expression of the child's inner nature, but rather a stark warning against adults who want to continue growing when they are grown: adult greed and adult ambition.

(And just to reiterate – because how can I not? – it is *David Cameron's favourite bedtime story.*)

'I meant no harm,' the Once-ler tells us, 'I most truly did not.' But he cannot claim ignorance – he repeatedly spurns the advice of the furry Lorax, who is both the voice of nature and, like Jiminy Cricket, his embodied conscience, and who warns him of the consequences of the smog and goo. The child listening is given a lesson in the gap between what adults say and what they do; between truths and excuses. The story happens in the space between the Once-ler's account and the picture they see of a forest reduced to stumps.

It is so bleak that environmental activist Naomi Klein, author of *This Changes Everything: Capitalism vs. the Climate*, has described how she read *The Lorax* to her two-year-old son, Toma, 'watched the terror cross his face' and decided, 'No, this is completely wrong.'

The story behind its creation perhaps explains its darkness. When she was fifty-five, Seuss's wife and long-time editorial collaborator, Helen, was diagnosed with

Guillain-Barré syndrome, which causes ascending paralysis. Seuss nursed her with Popsicles, and by setting up a series of mirrors so that she could see their dog waiting outside the window. She recovered enough to come home, but after that struggled for many years with health problems including a cancer diagnosis, as well as with Seuss's ongoing affair with Audrey Stone Dimond, a married woman eighteen years his junior. In 1967 Helen committed suicide with sodium pentobarbital capsules and was found in bed by their housekeeper. Her final letter began: 'Dear Ted, what has happened to us?'

It was signed off with their old code – the name of a made-up law firm: 'Grimalkin, Drouberhannus, Knalbner and Fepp'. (Such a terrible authority.)

Describing how he felt after her death, Seuss said: 'I didn't know whether to kill myself, burn the house down, or just go away and get lost.' In their home in La Jolla in San Diego over the next few years, he stared from his studio at a coast which had been unspoilt when he and Helen had arrived, but which now was cramped with condominiums. He hadn't been paying attention to its ruin. Writing seemed difficult, until a trip with Audrey to East Africa. He was at his swimming pool when he saw a group of elephants passing, and suddenly experienced a kind of 'release' that meant he scrawled 90 per cent of the book that afternoon. The trees of the Serengeti became Truffula Trees.

One can only assume his experience as a tourist in East Africa made him uneasy, as *The Lorax* is a book rank with guilt. It is also about an old man who cannot live his life again or undo his mistakes. The Once-ler lives in his shack, in the middle of the grim, polluted mess he made, trapped forever in his moment of *anagnorisis*, or tragic recognition, worrying his heart away. He will send down a 'Whisper-ma-phone' and tell his story for money, which he secretes in a hole in his glove. The story is a warning.

Finally, the Once-ler throws the reader the very last Truffula Seed. 'Catch!' he says. It looks like a pinprick of light. Unless they care enough to plant and nurture it, to grow a new forest 'nothing is going to get better'.

It is an awful responsibility, but all that Seuss can offer.

In a way it was a premonition. Isn't it all we too can offer, now, as we look into a darkening future; as Northern White Rhinos go the way of the Brown Bar-ba-loots and the sea chokes on needless plastics? Have the generations who could afford to make mistakes gone?

If we are the monsters, how can we teach our children to be something else?

There was once a father who slaughtered a pig, and his children saw that.

5. My Little Eye

On families lost and found

'What can he see?' the Ahlbergs ask of the little baby standing in his cot at the beginning of *Peepo!* (or *Peek-A-Boo!* in the US version). The hole in the facing page is almost the circle of his little eye, through which we can spy. Seeing and being seen is one of the great, profound subjects of toddler literature. Hiding and seeking; absence and presence.

Small children are notoriously terrible at knowing when they are hidden. 'Can you see me?' they ask, covering their eyes with their hands, while parents contemplate whether their children are absolute idiots. For a long time psychologists thought this was because they were egocentric, unable to imagine anyone else's perspective. More recently, though, experiments have suggested otherwise – Henrike Moll at the University of Southern California has observed that: 'young children consider mutual eye contact a requirement for one person to be able to see another.' (This is why they deem their little sister putting a tea towel over their head an effective strategy in a game of hide and seek.)

Sigmund Freud also famously observed how his grandson liked to play a game of making a cotton reel disappear and then reappear, throwing it out of his cot and forcing his mother to return it. Freud interpreted his babbles of 'ooh' and 'ah' as an attempt to say the German words *fort* (gone) and *da* (there). In *Beyond the Pleasure Principle*, Freud suggested that his grandson was re-enacting a scenario over which he had no control – his parent leaving him and then coming back – creating a sort of vengeful game in which he was now in charge. Compulsively repeating it was comforting; a way to re-assure himself of object permanence.

It is notable that the most beloved toy book mechanisms in picture books, the pop-up and the flap, allow a disappearance and then appearance to be acted out, over and over (and over and over and over) again. *Fort-da. Fort-da.*

In *Peepo!*, the father kissing the baby goodnight at the end is wearing his soldier's uniform, about to leave his child for months, or at the risk of forever.

*

Does the baby see that his father is going? The toddler peering at the book now is unlikely to register this underlying drama. Ahlberg has said: 'It's a mistake to think that a book for little children has to be like a glass of water so that every single element in it is accessible and clear and understood by a three-year-old.'

The question of what the child comprehends or doesn't is a recurring one in literature for small children. What is hidden in plain sight or simple words.

Take the earliest art form babies enjoy, the lullaby. They are listening, but it is probable that they are not understanding. Because of this there is a tension at the heart of them. Lorca has a stunning essay 'On Lullabies' which has the best description of a research process ever. (In A. S. Kline's translation, Lorca says: 'You will find me wherever a boy's ear opens, rosy and tender, or a girl's ear, white and fearfully awaiting the pin that pierces a hole for an earring.') Lorca speaks of how rhythm and repetition are needed to send the babe into a stupor, but 'no mother wants to be a snake-charmer'. It often feels as though the message of their soothing lulla-noises directly contradicts the darkness of the lyrics. 'When the bough breaks the cradle will fall . . .' 'There's a poor wee little lamby. / The bees and the butterflies pickin' at its eyes.' They superficially soothe, while actually articulating the 4 a.m. fear of the sleep-deprived women who composed them, many of whom must have lived in times of terrible infant mortality. Some seem weighted with anxious threats – some of the oldest surviving lullabies, from Babylon in 2000 BC, tell the baby off for disturbing the House God with crying.

In seventeenth-century Aragon they sang of the bogeyman: 'Sleep, child, sleep now ... Here comes the Coco and he will eat you'; while Kenyan women sing: 'rock, rock, the baby who cries will be eaten by a hyena.' There could even be a case made for some lullabies being the earliest poems of post-natal depression. Lorca argues that 'Spain utilizes its saddest melodies and most melancholy texts to tinge her children's first slumber', sung by mothers and poor, working-class wet nurses:

> This little turtle-dove
> Hasn't got a mother,
> A gipsy woman bore him
> And left him in a gutter.

Missing mothers. Missing fathers. Daddy's gone a-hunting.

When Gruff was born I decided to find a lullaby I liked online and learn it by heart to sing to him. During my research I stumbled on a BBC World Service documentary, *The Language of Lullabies*, which argued that in every culture the signature inflections of the mother tongue are carried in lullabies, and that their frequent use of 6/8 time mimics the movement of the womb. It also featured a snatch of an old Manx song I spent an afternoon memorizing. It was not as dark as many others, but was still about going and returning; our loved ones needing to be both wild and to come home:

> Oh hush thee my dove, oh hush thee my rowan,
> Oh hush thee my lapwing, my little brown bird.

Oh fold thy wings and seek thy nest now,
Oh shine the berry on the bright tree,
The bird is home from the mountain and valley.
Oh horo hi ri ri. Cadul gu lo.

Fort-da, fort-da.

The first books with moving paper parts were for adults, not children. Benedictine monk Matthew Paris used volvelles (rotatable wheel charts) to help monks calculate holy days in his thirteenth-century *Chronica Majora*. The device was later used to teach anatomy and astrology. Landscape architect Capability Brown used flaps to illustrate before-and-after views of his gardens, while Thomas Malton's *Compleat Treatise on Perspective, in Theory and Practice; on the True Principles of Dr. Brook Taylor* (1775) is the first known commercially produced pop-up book, with three-dimensional shapes pulled up by strings to teach perspective.

Some of the first three-dimensional and tab-activated books designed to entertain children were produced by Lothar Meggendorfer in Germany during the nineteenth century. Sendak has said of him: 'he was the supreme master of animation; every gesture, both animal and human, coarse and refined, was conveyed via the limited but, in his hands, versatile technique of moveable paper parts.' Such books, though, were for an elite audience. It was only in 1929, when British book publisher S. Louis Giraud began producing 'living models' that sprang up automatically when the book was opened, moderately priced and printed on coarse, inexpensive paper, that a mass-market version of these intricate machines became available. They quickly became extremely popular, especially after, in 1930s New York, Blue Ribbon Publishing managed to find an even more commercial model. They animated Walt Disney characters with 'pop-ups', inventing the term.

The first time you read a pop-up with a child, it is full of wonderful surprises, every line seemingly loaded with exclamation marks. Every page is a jack-in-the-box; a dancer springing out of a cake. They squeal as the shark lurches for them or the ghost jumps out; coo over the fireworks and bouquets. Afterwards, by the fourth or fifth time, the game is to re-enact the surprise: *eeek, ooooh, wow!* The pleasure is in repeating the little drama of reading.

The flap book is similar, but somehow even more satisfying (and pleasingly for the parent, the mechanisms are not so delicate and easily broken, or at least are more easily fixable with Sellotape than a pop-up book's elaborately structured toucan beaks or meerkat pyramids). *Dear Zoo* (1982) by Rod Campbell is a favourite in our house – so pleasurable for the child in the way they get to be a finickity consumer, constantly sending back their gifts to the zoo (the lion is too fierce; the elephant is too heavy; the frog is too jumpy) rather than having to smile and say thank you for whatever ugly, unsuitable present a relative has regifted. But the ultimate flap book, the one that really popularized the genre, is *Where's Spot?* (1980) by Eric Hill.

Hill was born in Holloway, North London, in 1927. Aged just twelve he was an evacuee, sent to the small village of Bluntisham, though he returned to London that Christmas and stayed for the rest of the war. Perhaps this early experience of being removed from his family and then reunited with them influenced the central plotline of *Where's Spot?* Something in its story of a mother trying to find her son chimes on a deep, emotional level with toddlers.

The Blitz left its impact on Hill. Quitting school at fourteen to work as an errand boy in an art studio, he was encouraged to draw cartoons and particularly enjoyed copying aeroplanes. Later he did a stint with the Royal Air Force, posted in Germany. Hill has described Spot as a golden retriever puppy 'with a mix of hound to provide the characteristic markings' but has also observed that: 'It must have been subconscious but I realized that when I came to draw the spot on his body and the tip of his tail I was copying the markings on an aircraft.'

Like Dick Bruna with Miffy, Eric Hill always aimed for a simplicity that made his puppy a 'ready-made trademark of its kind'. He began each drawing with a black pen outline, then used a brush dipped in watercolour inks to produce an almost flat colour. He chose the typeface – Century Schoolbook Infant – and, at first, said pictures of Spot should only be placed against a white background. It was the flaps, though, that made *Where's Spot?* such an innovative book. Hill was a graphic designer working on advertising flyers with a 'lift-the-flap' feature when his two-year-old son, Christopher, watched one work and delightedly demanded he 'Do it again!' Though flaps had occasionally been used in more elaborate 'toy books', no one had aimed them at the youngest market, with the simple format of one flap per spread they could open themselves. His innovation allowed babies too young to understand language to interact with books.

Although Spot is, of course, a great pun (because you have to spot him), it is seemingly a hard one to translate, so Hill allowed flexibility in translation, letting common puppy names from each country be used. The adventures of Spot have since been translated into 65 languages, including Inupiaq, Occitan, Frisian and Faroese, and his names include Dribbel (the Netherlands), Fleck (Germany), Korochan (Japan), and Smot (Welsh). In the dog-loving UK he has become a national treasure – a recent study by Millward Brown reported that Spot had 99 per cent awareness amongst UK parents and 83 per cent amongst children.

Many Spot books followed the first, which is still the best. *Where's Spot?* is full of surreal, surprising details: the tables have cabriole legs; a crocodile snaps 'No' beneath the bed's valance; the piano is a pink baby grand with a hippo inside. On the other hand, it's just a recognizable, homely story about a mother and child playing hide and seek, with the added narrative urgency that his dinner is going cold and his mum is starting to think he is 'naughty' for hiding. The child can both 'help' his mother to find Spot and help Spot to be found.

(Having said that, I always assumed it was quite a liberal household because Spot's mum is known by her first name, Sally.)

*

Hide and seek is a kind of hunt. Perhaps, long ago, it was training for that – for the boys who needed to learn how to hide from a predator, to creep up on a rabbit or a deer? Another interesting book about family and finding is Michael Rosen and Helen Oxenbury's *We're Going on a Bear Hunt* (1989). Interestingly, the text is, almost verbatim, an American children's song that Rosen would perform as part of his poetry readings (it's also sometimes a lion hunt). Asked to turn it into a book, Rosen lengthened it with a forest and snowstorm and a few more juicy onomatopoeic phrases (swishy swashy), but left it largely unchanged. His original manuscript, in the Seven Stories Archive, has 'retold by Michael Rosen' at the top, though in the edition I have the publishers seem to have quietly dropped this, keen to suggest that it is Rosen's own work (and therefore in copyright, I suppose).

The genius of the book, Rosen has generously admitted, lies in the illustrator Helen Oxenbury's interpretation of the text. He originally envisioned a King, Queen and Jester and the manuscript, larded with Tippex, is full of stage directions suggesting a conga of people, swaggering, etc., yet Oxenbury seems to have ignored these entirely. Instead she has drawn a family, based on her own children, seeking the bear through a very English landscape. When Rosen first saw the watercolours he 'couldn't figure out what they had to do with a bear hunt. It looked like a family having a holiday in Cornwall.'

Most readers, myself included, see a father on the cover with his three children, but though Oxenbury describes him as 'the dad' in a 1989 interview with Leonard

S. Marcus, she has since said the tallest figure was meant to be her eldest son, admitting: 'I actually failed to make him look like a young teenager.' Chanting the rhyme, our little gang pass through mudflats, a forest, fields, and a beach with a cave Oxenbury based on Druidstone in Pembrokeshire. This is a land in which bears were long ago hunted to extinction. The rhyme is just play: a walking song, used to persuade the younger ones to continue the adventure ('Oh no! We've got to go through it!'). The last thing they actually expect to encounter is an *actual* bear.

But then there it is, with four exclamation marks !!!!

Of course, they're not actually capable of killing (they're middle class!). The family run back – through snow, woods, mud, fields, river – with the illustrations brilliantly becoming like a strip cartoon to reflect the acceleration of the text. They pile into the house (shutting the door just in time) and plunge under the thick, pink covers of their bed.

There, the baby picks up its teddy – the bear of human imagining – and smiles with delight. The real bear, shoulders slumped, heads back to its lonely cave. As T. S. Eliot observed: 'Humankind cannot bear very much reality.' (Not a pun, I promise.) In seeking and hiding, the family unit has been reinforced, and the outsider has served its purpose.

Owl Babies (1992), written by Martin Waddell and illustrated by Patrick Benson, also explores family relationships through absence and presence. Waddell has spoken interestingly about how 'animals are used in picture books because you can make them do things that you wouldn't be able to let children do', and in *Owl Babies* the babies are put in a situation that would be impossible to depict in the human world without the mother being reported to social services. They wake in a dark wood and find she has gone, leaving them entirely alone. With their podgy bodies, stumpy wings and flattened, big-eyed faces owls make the perfect avian substitute for toddlers (hence their ubiquity in books such as *I'm Not Scared* and *WOW! Said the Owl*). The three owl babies each react differently, with Sarah trying to be grown-up and sensible, Percy not really helping, and little Bill only able to utter the desperate refrain: 'I want my mummy!'

The pictures are densely, delicately inked in a way that makes their home – a hole in a trunk – feel vividly, warmly woody. I'm always struck by the few precise details: the cosiness of the twigs and leaves mixed in with their own 'owl feathers'. Patrick Benson has spoken of how when he first read the text he felt 'unnerved by the prospect of having to draw several pictures of baby owls having a long chat' but he managed it by thinking like a director, zooming in and out and changing perspective. He also credited Amelia Edwards at Walker Books for much of the book's beauty. She suggested drawing images in black ink on white paper 'leaving a black area out of which the text would be reversed', then transferring the drawings to clear acetate so he could paint the colour 'on a new sheet of paper, very loosely with watercolours'. This was doubly clever, both making the production of foreign language editions easy and allowing 'a really rich, lustrous black finish as the black plate was not affected by an overlay of colour'.

The darkness feels palpable.

The interest of the book lies in the question of what your mother does when she's not with you. It is a thought experiment many small children have barely attempted, yet the owl babies spend most of the pages pondering this. Is she hunting? Is she getting them treats ('mice and things that are nice' in Sarah's rhyming phrase)? Is she lost? Has she been caught by a fox?

The spread on which the Owl Mother returns shows this, beautifully, from a vantage point high in the tree-tops. We see her swooping back towards her babies, who are in the distance with their backs to her, not yet aware their ordeal is over. It says simply, with heartfelt relief: 'And she came.' Waddell has spoken of how originally there was much more text: 'They were the best lines I wrote, but when I saw the image I knew they were redundant.'

Behind every story, a different story.

Martin Waddell was born in Belfast in 1941. Just before the Blitz, Waddell's family moved to Newcastle, County Down, beneath the Mountains of Mourne. As a child, life in the area was idyllic, populated by animals and folktales. After his parents split in the 1950s, he moved to London where he signed for Fulham F. C. before realizing he was not going to be able to make his living as a professional footballer. When he turned his hand to writing he found immediate success with a comic thriller, *Otley*, made into a film starring Tom Courtenay. Then, in 1969, he married Rosaleen, and they settled back in County Down, at Donaghadee.

Waddell has described, in an interview with *The Independent*, how, following the birth of his second son in 1972, a life-altering event occurred. His young family now lived opposite a Catholic church, and the local UDA would often perform their drill in the street outside. One evening, after he saw a gang of kids hurrying away from the church, Waddell entered the vestry to investigate and saw 'what looked like a wasp's nest on a chair. The "nest" lit up.' It was a bomb. His first thought after he regained consciousness was that his family were dead. For months afterwards, he would wake up screaming.

For six years, such was the 'total body shock' he suffered, Waddell couldn't work, so ended up looking after his three small sons at home. In the winter of 1972, they rented a dilapidated house on a rock overlooking the sea, its kitchen often ankle-deep in water. He has said that he was 'given a privilege which very few fathers have: the day-to-day business of looking after the kids. This didn't feel very much like a privilege at the time but it actually led to the richest vein of my own work.' He thought of moving far away but felt too deeply attached to County Down. He watched his children grow up where he had grown up, and where all his stories are set, at the foot of the Mourne Mountains: his precious, vulnerable, only home.

In 1978 the writing somehow returned. His father

had always told him that 'writing books will butter you no parsnips', but Waddell began to draw on his experiences as a father to write picture books. By 1988, when his *Can't You Sleep, Little Bear?* (illustrated by Barbara Firth) won the Smarties Prize, he was an 'overnight success'. *Farmer Duck* (1991) followed, with pictures by Helen Oxenbury, which she pithily sums up as 'a sort of *Animal Farm* . . . for babies'. Then came *Owl Babies*.

Waddell has claimed it was written in about three hours after an event in a local supermarket. He came across a small, scared girl standing absolutely still, repeating over and over, 'I want my mummy!' They found her mother eventually, and Waddell had found a story.

When she returns, the Owl Mother wants to know why there is so much fuss. 'You knew I'd come back.' It is, on one level, a comforting tale, used to reassure children with separation anxiety that they are being irrational.

But of course, on another level, Waddell knows their fear is not irrational. And anyway, what *was* the mother doing? When talking about the book with my friend Hannah, she said that her son is always indignant that the mother doesn't bring back nice juicy mice in her beak. What force of nature made the owl leave her children, then? From what truth is she protecting them? Foxes do indeed prowl outside. The UDA practise; nests explode; wives and babies perish. The father who wakes screaming and the child who shrieks for her mummy both share the same terror.

*

One of my first memories is of being without my mother for a few days. When pregnant with my sister, my mum had a threatened miscarriage and went into hospital, so my dad fended for us as well as he could by taking me to the chippy. I would only have been one and a half. I can picture the bottles of Space Special and Dandelion & Burdock. The lady there gave me two chips wrapped in a scrap of greaseproof paper, which I ate on the dry-stone wall outside, my father saying: 'What are we going to do, eh?' (But he must have told me this, surely.)

Anecdotally, other people's first memories often seem triggered by a shock – a fall; the sight of blood; a seagull snatching a sandwich. Perhaps my trigger was the shock of my mother not being around. Most of the time she was a constant. She was patient, tireless, and always, I now recognize, generous enough to scream as if genuinely startled when I popped out of the linen basket with the wicker lid on my head, like one of Ali Baba's Forty Thieves. She was pretty, warm, tatty-nailed. Her hair changed a lot in those years, from blonde to brown to red, as if she was trying to work out how a mum should look. In my memory we are on her bed and I am balanced on her bare feet like an acrobat; she is opening an oven door and pulling out a tray of rock cakes, with their sweet singed smell.

There was a time, though, when everything was subtly different. My Uncle Paul – my mother's brother – had a terrible accident when hang-gliding. He was brain-damaged, in a coma for weeks before he died; there but gone. I remember sitting with my father in the car outside the hospital as she visited him. I remember the phone ringing one night, after a dark drive home from my grandparents' house in Salford. My mum answered and began to howl.

I was too young to attend the funeral. I knew, that day, I had to be kind to my mum when she came back. But what about the other days? For me, Uncle Paul was just a couple of memories – a handsome, charismatic man who had sat in our living room; slightly intimidating, obviously special. How could I know the gnawing absence grief leaves? What it means for your brother to hide from you forever, where you can never, ever find him?

In the months afterwards, I recall my Grandad Cranshaw, who usually giddily tickled us saying he was 'Mr Croc', nursing his anger. I recall my mother having a couple of furious tantrums; once leaping out of a moving car. After our first holiday abroad to Spain, finding our photos hadn't come out, she smashed the camera on the kitchen floor, stamping and screaming like Rumpelstiltskin until it was irredeemably broken. I never joined the dots between these episodes and loss until recently.

A couple of times, she declared to my sister and me that she was so sick of something she was going to run away with the gypsies. The only gypsies I knew were the raggle-taggle ones in Hilda Boswell's *Treasury of Poetry*, in which the Lady's heart 'melted away as snow' to hear them singing. My mother always read that poem aloud to us with such passion, especially when the Lady, leaving her Lord for the gypsies, asks: 'What care I for a goose-feather bed, / With the sheet turned down so bravely, O?'

In the pictures, the Lady is loose-haired, bare-footed under a sky luminous with dusk. This was my mother's vision of herself free from domesticity; from responsibilities. From all that caring.

After a while, my mother declaring she would run away with the gypsies became a half-joke. She sometimes added that she might eat baked hedgehog. Typing this, another vague memory comes back – hedgehog-flavoured crisps. Can that be right? My father bringing them back in that sack of different-flavoured crisps taped around his classroom . . . It's surely an untrustworthy memory. (I am writing a memoir of the time before I was five, I remind myself. They are all untrustworthy memories. The whole project is absurd.)

It is six o'clock, which is dinner-and-show time in our house. I know, I know, they shouldn't be so used to TV dinners (no lectures, please). The children slurp noodles; Daddy Pig is failing to put up a picture. I google hedgehog crisps and there they are: *1981 . . . Inspired by the old gypsy stories of baking hedgehog . . . actually pork fat and herbs . . .*

Bizarrely, the Office of Fair Trading took the manufacturers to court on a charge of false advertising, and they ended up having to interview gypsies who'd eaten actual hedgehog in order to make them taste more hedgehoggy.

A share of the profits went to a wildlife hospital called St Tiggywinkles.

*

Distraction, of course, is another type of absence, too easy now in this time of mobile phones; of parents doing an online Ocado shop while their children cause chaos in the ball-pool. Distracted mothers are still fairly rare in picture books, although there is Bernard's mother and that woman in Sendak's *Outside Over There*, catatonic, gazing numbly out to sea while (in one of the most chilling picture book images of all time) the goblins abduct her baby and replace it with one 'made all of ice'. Mrs Large, in Jill Murphy's series about an elephant family, is unusual in being depicted as an individual with her own needs which are often separate from her family's. She wants to lose weight, go out for the evening, have 'five minutes' peace' in the bath with a piece of leftover cake – but she is always dragged, largely cheerfully, back into the fray.

Mainly, it is fathers who are distracted. Author and illustrator Anthony Browne's *Gorilla* (1983) is perhaps the most disturbing depiction of a father absent even when he is in the house. It is a story about a young girl, Hannah, who has never seen a gorilla yet is obsessed by them: drawing them, watching them, reading about them. Her father seems to be her only parent (the breakfast table is set for two). Has the mother abandoned them? Died? The atmosphere seems heavy with grief. Hannah, though, is not yearning for her lost mum but for her dad. When he is with her, her father holds up his broadsheet newspaper like a wall, as cold as the fridge behind him. In the evenings he works at his desk with his back to her, always too busy to be bothered. The gorilla seems to represent the male figure she yearns for:

strong, protective, flesh and blood. Browne has explained his repeated use of apes by noting: 'My dad was a boxer so he had this fierce, physical presence . . . he was a big man, but kindly, and gorillas are like that: powerful, capable of aggression, but mostly gentle, sensitive.'

The book emerged, for Browne, from a childhood memory of longing for a real trumpet, but only being given a plastic toy one and being deeply disappointed. Hannah longs for a real gorilla for her birthday but her father only gets her a toy. Then, in the night, it grows into a huge, tender giant – a hulking, smiling beast who puts on her father's coat and swings her off through the treetops for a trip to the zoo.

It is such a sad book. Even the page on which Hannah and the gorilla dance on the lawn and we are told 'Hannah had never been so happy' can make me start to well up. All she wants is a few bright moments of attention. She is dancing a clumsy waltz, her feet on the gorilla's feet. He is leaving soon. The chimpanzees in the zoo, too, their wrinkled faces pressed against the bars, are 'beautiful. But sad.'

Home is a cage for Hannah and her father. Everything in the kitchen is patterned with a check like a cage. The wallpaper in her father's study has vertical stripes like bars. We see Hannah through the metal bars of her bed.

Work is a cage. Masculinity is a cage. Loss is a cage.

Anthony Browne grew up in his grandparents' pub near Bradford, which he remembers as 'cramped, dark, cold, and pretty rough – working-class men drinking Tetley's bitter, which was known as "fighting beer". My dad watered it down, but it didn't stop the fighting.' Their mother once made the mistake of mentioning she hated her name Doris, and was teasingly referred to by her sons as 'Our Doris' ever after. His father had seen harrowing things in the Second World War; had killed German guards with his bare hands. A gentle man, he was traumatized by what he had done. One day he wrestled a vacuum cleaner to the floor, mistaking it for a German. Still, he had won a Military Cross in North Africa, and Browne and his brother Michael saw their father as a hero whom they wanted to emulate. He liked to draw and acted every year in the local pantomime.

On Easter Monday when he was seventeen, Browne's father died in front of him. His heart had been damaged by rheumatic fever as a child, so was known to be weak, but Browne had refused to think about it. Then one day his father was mending a plug when suddenly he fell as if in slow motion, and started to writhe. He frothed at the mouth. In his biography *Playing the Shape Game*, co-written with his son, Browne describes with awful honesty how his mother began 'hopeless, uneducated resuscitation procedures ... mimicking the histrionic gestures of TV doctors'. Finally: 'he was just lying there: this great, god-like figure on the floor, amid this scene of total devastation. I'd thought he was invincible . . .'

If *Gorilla* seems, in some way, to express anger at the failures of fathers, it ends with a moment of redemption. Throughout the pages of *Gorilla* red is Hannah's colour – the colour of her top, her boots, the gorilla's bow tie, the favourite foods she orders when, after the zoo, the gorilla takes her to a café for a slap-up birthday feed (ketchup, raspberries, cakes and sundaes topped with shining cherries). On her birthday morning her dad is wearing red too, and he holds her shoulders. It is a moment of connection. They have found each other. There is, we notice, a banana in his back pocket.

Browne's own encounter with the largest living primate didn't end so well. He was asked to present a programme on picture books, and the producer thought it would make good TV for him to meet his first gorilla. Unfortunately, the zoo owner had fought with the TV company about payment, and, as Browne went in, the zoo owner threw rose petals into the cage. 'These are like sweets for gorillas,' Browne has recounted. 'They get very excited. And the first gorilla came up to me and suddenly sank her teeth into my calf. It was the most excruciating pain I've ever felt.'

The leg of his jeans turned black with blood.

In their 2005 study 'Gender Role Stereotyping of Parents in Children's Picture Books: The Invisible Father', David A. Anderson and Mykol Hamilton looked at a sample of 200 picture books including Caldecott winners, best-sellers, and New York Public Library's list of 'books everyone should know' and concluded that:

Mothers were shown more often than fathers as caring nurturers who discipline their children and express a full range of emotions. Fathers were under-represented and portrayed as relatively stoic actors who took little part in the lives of their children.

And if the fathers we expose our preschoolers to are not distracted or absent, they are often incompetent like Daddy Pig – progenitor of a thousand think-pieces called 'What Peppa Pig Tells Us About British Fatherhood' – who can't even flip a pancake, read a map or do a couple of press-ups, and is the butt of family jokes (the password to get into Peppa's tree house is 'Daddy's Big Tummy') – or the clumsy elephant Mr Large, who can't run the house for a day without a series of domestic disasters in Jill Murphy's *Mr Large In Charge*.

Papa Bear, from the Berenstain Bear series by Jan and Stan Berenstain, was the first of the slapstick dads. He is almost over-present and irritatingly competitive; always pontificating or showing off, with terrible consequences. Theodor Geisel (Dr Seuss himself) helped edit their first book for Random House's 'Beginner Books' imprint. He was a stringent editor, telling the Berenstains that their first book had too many 'convenience' rhymes which didn't add to the narrative and their line lengths were 'all over the place'. In *The Big Honey Hunt* (1962) Papa Bear refuses to go to the store for honey as Mama Bear has suggested, and instead ends up taking his son on a wild chase where they encounter skunks, a porcupine and a swarm of bees before ending up in a river. 'There are already too many bears,' Seuss warned them. 'Sendak's got some kind of a bear. There's Yogi

Bear, the Three Bears, Smokey Bear, the Chicago Bears.' The Berenstains ignored him and over 200 books followed, many of which follow the same plot beats – Papa tries to teach his son to cycle and there are a series of embarrassing accidents, etc. In my favourite, *The Bears' Picnic* (1966), Papa Bear keeps swearing he will find a better picnic spot but leads them into a biblical plague of mosquitos; a rubbish dump; an exposed clifftop during a storm (they end up picnicking in their house at the dining table).

The formula has been boiled down by the Berenstains themselves as follows: 'Papa sets out to instruct Small Bear in some aspect of the art of living and ends up badly the worse for wear, with Small Bear expressing his appreciation for the fine lesson Papa has taught him.' The main lesson, then, is schooling children in sarcasm. Over time the Berenstains tried various defences of Papa Bear, including the fact that his 'bullheadedness' was based on Stan's own. 'It's a comedy cliché,' Stan suggested. 'It's The Honeymooners ... It's vaudeville.' Also, Mama Bear mainly stays at home with an apron on because female bears are apparently 'terrifyingly good mothers' while the male ones 'make lousy fathers'. Behind Papa Bear and all the fools who follow him, though, is the implication that a father's parenting skills somehow matter less. To portray a mother in the same way would seem horrifically cruel, because it would be to attack (wouldn't it?) her entire sense of self.

In our house, it should be said, though, it was my mum whom we compared to Papa Bear, with her endless spot-picking. And my father was, for his generation, a very present father – teachers didn't have such long hours then and he was pretty efficient with his preparation, always back soon after 3.30 p.m., around in the summer holidays. He didn't mind hoovering, pushing prams, washing up (although he always sang, to the tune of Scott Walker's 'Make It Easy On Yourself': 'Washing up is so very hard to DOO-ooOO-ooOO'), polishing the coffee table (daily, a touch of obsessiveness again). He liked to keep a diary, recording our family's little victories.

My husband Richard and I share the bedtime reading. I have been consciously looking for books with better fathers in them, but there aren't many. *Peck Peck Peck* by Lucy Cousins (of Maisy fame) is lovely – after a woodpecker teaches his son to peck, the little woodpecker pecks holes in literally everything he comes across that day (a teddy bear and Jane Eyre, shampoo and the loo, margarine and seventeen jelly beans) until he's made himself dizzy. In the end, rather than disciplining him as you might expect, the father is full of pride, saying 'that's fantastic' and then pecking him with kisses. *Some Dogs Do* by Jez Alborough features a father whose belief in his son lifts him up. Then there is Martin Waddell and Barbara Firth's *Can't You Sleep, Little Bear?* Anthony Browne's *My Dad* ('He's alright, my dad'). A handful of others – but each is, you feel, slightly aware of itself as an anomaly.

When I think of picture books that show the reality of family life, Shirley Hughes would be near the top of my list. She catches the texture of the everyday with a young family like no one else – lost keys, 'wild white washing' on the line, crusts on the floor, dens made from blankets draped over furniture, wet socks, little cars left out in the garden, fridges messy with magnets. Annie Rose slides around on her potty and Bernard blows bubbles in jelly. Hughes works in gouache, which has more body than watercolour, and works hard at keeping the energy of her rough sketches, finishing by 'crisping up' detail with a very sharp pencil. Her pictures have the spontaneity and slight ugliness of reality; its dirty surfaces. The mothers are kind and slightly frazzled, like the mum in *Alfie Gets in First* who brings the shopping in then goes out to unstrap Annie Rose from the buggy and ends up locked out with Alfie inside. It's an incredibly clever picture book – Hughes uses the 'gutter' down the middle to represent the door – and manages to capture the kind of domestic dramas that make up preschool life, both incredibly minor and yet remembered forever, in a way few others are. She reminds me these small moments are the moments of our lives.

Hughes's own family life, as a child, featured an often-absent father. She was brought up with her two older sisters in the 'posh' suburbs of Liverpool, a city that was both the source of her family's wealth and a place of great poverty, and where she saw young women who had lost all their teeth from rickets and 'a man with a barrow selling bricks for people to hurl through the windows of Irish people'. Hughes's father was T. J. Hughes, who ran a chain of well-known department stores. He worked thirteen-hour days and she recalls him being 'nice when I met him'. But in 1932 his health began to suffer due to depression and he was said to have 'retired'. Her son, the journalist Ed Vulliamy, has written that 'what actually happened is one of the roaring silent stories in a city usually so assertive about its history' – T. J. Hughes found that, after taking time off, control of the business had been taken away from him. 'My grandfather boarded the Liverpool–Dublin ferry for a trip he had planned and was never seen again.'

Hughes's father absented himself for all time then, his body lost to the vast grey waters.

Asked whether she would include darker subjects in her children's books, Hughes has answered: 'I don't think you should inflict this stuff on young children, you've got to give them the idea that the world is a pretty nice place and it's very interesting rather more than to watch out in case something awful happens, that's for later.'

Soon afterwards the war came. Hughes remembers how: 'My mother, quite a shy person, went from sitting in her nice garden with the maid bringing her tea to being this hard-pressed figure wearing an overcoat inside because it was so cold.' She recalls that: 'It was a very tough time. Children today think the war was daring but, in fact, if you lived at home it was just deadly boring . . . You really had to amuse yourself, so I did a lot of drawing.' After it was over, desperate to escape the class-conscious suburbs with their pressure to get engaged (her eldest sister married young), Hughes moved to London, where she rented a freezing bedsit and hawked her portfolio around the city's publishers with little success.

After marrying the architect John Vulliamy in 1952, Hughes settled in Notting Hill and they began a family. Hughes has described those early years with small children as a time of 'crushing responsibility', but she was observing and sketching, even as she felt that illustrators like Quentin Blake were overtaking her while she was in the 'pram lane'. Her first book as an author-illustrator, *Lucy & Tom's Day*, appeared only in 1960. It is, fittingly, a story about her great subject – siblings.

It is telling that my memories begin with discovering, through her hospitalization, that my mother was pregnant with my sister. Perhaps it caused a kind of fall into history; the realization that things would change and keep changing. The arrival of a sibling is ultimate *peeka-boo*; nine months of hushed crouching in the belly then up they pop. It is a fraught moment for both the older child and the parents, with a whole section of the picture book market dedicated to getting the elder sibling into the right mental space (and making money from parental anxiety) via the 'new baby' genre: *There's Going to Be a Baby*; *Waiting for Baby*; *There's a House inside my Mummy*; *Mummy, Mummy, What's in Your Tummy?*; *Where Did that Baby Come From?*; *I Love you Baby*; *Hello Baby*; *Welcome Baby*; *I Just Couldn't Wait to Meet You*; *The New Small Person*; *My Baby Sister*; *My Little Brother*; *I'm a New*

Big Brother; *I'm a New Big Sister*. The commercial imperative is clear in the way most franchises have shoehorned in a baby book – *Mr Men: My Sister*; *Spot's Baby Sister*; *Guess How Much I Love You: My Baby Book*; *Babar and the New Baby*; *Angelina and the New Baby*; *Topsy and Tim – The New Baby*; *Miffy and the New Baby*; *The Berenstain Bears' New Baby*.

There are a couple of titles that seem to treat the enormity of the situation with appropriate gravitas, such as Anthony Browne's *Changes*, in which the boy's anxieties are hinted at in background images – a TV screen shows a cuckoo forcing baby sparrows out of their nest. Mainly, though, the books are masterpieces of euphemism, as is *The Birds and the Bees and the Berenstain Bears* by Jan and Stan Berenstain that declares, archly: 'When a mama bear's lap slowly disappears / she has some special news to tell her little dears!' Plot-wise, the actual psychological drama – the usurpation and betrayal – is deliberately downplayed to the point of tedium. Miffy paints a picture of some chicks and, showing rather advanced crafting skills, makes a blue wool mouse (presumably for the baby but this is not specified), holds the baby on her knee, then gets to take cake to school. Small Bear helps his father to make him a new bigger bed. Sharing your parents with a demanding new person is treated as one of the lesser occasions, like a wobbly tooth or pancake day.

When I was pregnant with Cate, I dutifully read these to Gruff. I was trying to use them, I suppose, as what the writer Julia Donaldson dismisses as 'picture-book medicine: if I read this book three times a day to her then she might go to school and smile and overcome all her own problems.' When Gruff showed little interest, I worried that he wasn't worried; that he had no idea what upheaval was coming.

When his sister Cate was eventually born, he seemed basically fine with it, but I was not – two was exhausting, impossible, and I felt that every moment I wasn't breastfeeding I had to lavish him with attention so he wouldn't be jealous; so he wouldn't be one of those children who you're afraid to leave in a room with your baby. You know, the ones you've heard about who gouge and pull; push pillows into faces to 'make baby quiet'.

The second pregnancy had harrowed my body. My first felt like a blossoming; the second a grim process of entropy. Cystitis, piles, varicose veins, my first grey hairs. The first months too were less miraculous this time, more simply anxious. It was the summer of Brexit. Our pet fish began to die – Bing I, Bang II, Bong I – slowing and struggling until it was sickening to watch their gills gasp and we had to throw them in the bin. Gruff broke his foot on his scooter; he was given a blue cast that began to smell in the heat. That week the whole family took worming tablets. The nights were clammy, and Cate slept beside us in our bedroom, in a Moses basket balanced on a coffee table, zipped into a tiny sleeping bag. If Richard was out and the window was open I would be certain with every siren (there are a lot of sirens in Peckham) that uniformed men were coming to my door with terrible news (*do not ask for whom the siren wails; it wails for you*).

I breastfed that year in the thin blue light of Twitter trolling on my iPhone. Update, uphate. When her head slumped I'd lay her back down but couldn't switch off myself. In the dark, drained, sweating beneath the curdled duvet, I would hear the mice begin to move. Small pink claws scratching against wood, a horror-movie sound effect like undead nails scraping a coffin lid. A scuttle that moved along the skirting boards, making me taut with attention. I imagined them somehow crawling up into the basket of my sleeping baby daughter, dirty, twitching. Pissing in bedding. Teeth testing her cheek.

We laid cruel, cheap traps under the bed, baited with peanut butter crackers, but night after night nothing snapped them into silence, they came and soiled the dark, made me listen to every squeak and breath of hers or theirs.

And as I lay awake my worries ricocheted between the world and the mice and Gruff – how he was coping or not, how he seemed to sense something had shifted. His thrashing tantrum in that lift at his auntie's wedding.

His trembling-lipped *no, no*, when I sang her the first verse of that lullaby: 'O hush thee, my love.'

The siblings in Shirley Hughes's books are a model and a comfort, always tolerant of each other, fondly muddling through. Tom and Lucy, Katie and Olly, *My Naughty Little Sister*, Alfie and Annie Rose. Then, of course, there are Joe, Dave and older sister Bella in *Dogger*.

Dogger is another tale of lost and found, one that can be read over and over as a reassurance. *Fort-da. Fort-da.* It is based on a real toy that belonged to Shirley's son Ed. The original Dogger can be seen in the documentary *Shirley Hughes – What Do Artists Do All Day?* with his bald patches and distinct, single, upturned ear – stuck that way from being slept against so much. Dogger is not just a bedtime 'cuddler' (as we say in our house) but a constant playmate, being dragged around on string or wrapped in blankets. Eventually, Dave leaves Dogger somewhere. (It is not stated explicitly, but the pictures seem to suggest that Dave leaves Dogger poking through the school railings. He is distracted by an ice-cream van, then giving his little brother Joe 'in-between licks' of his melty pink cornet.)

The school fair comes, along with a series of delightfully nostalgic illustrations that explain the book's enduring charm ('nearly new' stalls, a lucky-dip barrel, a fancy-dress parade with a Dalek, a wheelbarrow race where half the wheelbarrows' faces look smushed). Bella wins an alarmingly large teddy with a blue silk bow in the raffle. But then Dave sees Dogger on the toy stall where he can't afford the 5p price tag. He can't find Mum and Dad, only, eventually, Bella – but by then Dogger has been bought, and the girl won't sell him back. Dave cries and cries.

'Then Bella did something *very* kind.'

Jesus, it made me start to weep just typing that out.

Bella swaps her giant teddy with the blue bow for Dogger.

Just look at how Hughes has caught Bella's stance, as she awkwardly but solemnly accepts Dave's grateful hug. She tells Dave she won't miss the big teddy: 'Anyway, if I had another teddy in my bed there wouldn't be room for me.'

Those first weeks pass.

One bright afternoon I'd just got Cate to nap and was adjusting the nipple pads when I finally saw a mouse stare sweetly up at me from the floor, harmless as the design on a nursery curtain. The next night the trap broke its neck. Cate began to sleep through and moved into a cot in the next room, and Gruff gave her his Igglepiggle to cuddle.

Better slept, my fears receded: I watched my children grow fond of each other.

I don't understand, now, why I feared otherwise, as I always adored my own little sister. Mary had hair a shade darker than mine, brighter eyes, and a smaller, dirtier nose which she rubbed with a fist. She was altogether more elfin than me (perhaps our Welsh genes). In photos she always grinned daftly, scrunched or gurning, an adorable gargoyle. Freckles smeared her lip. Like my father, she tipped towards obsessive: counting jelly sweets in jars, testing boundaries, repeatedly making teddies do the V sign. She was never more his daughter than when we had our annual Grand National buffet of picnic eggs and cream cakes, and every one of her cuddly toys received a betting slip (the winner was tucked into her bed that night). We got on well, because we accepted our assigned roles – knowing I was serious and bookish, Mary decided to be sociable and sporty. She got cute and funny; I took patient and wise.

In *Dogger*, of course I am the older sister. I liked giving Mary toys she would enjoy more than me, like my Sylvanian Families mole. Does my throat catch then at my own kindness? Perhaps, but it's for something else too.

However much you love an adult, they must bear their struggles and sadnesses themselves. Sometimes you must accept you cannot help; sometimes they are bent on destroying themselves and you cannot stop them. But when you love a small child, for a little while at least, their joy can be entirely within your gift. I know this now as a mother but learnt it first as a big sister. It's so simple: a bubble, a tickle, a lolly, a wriggly worm, a toy lost then found. Happy endings cost a few pence, are two-a-penny.

What luck it is, *Dogger* reminds us, to live in such days.

6. The Glass Castle

On fairy tales and femininity

In a cottage at the edge of a forest, a poor widow lived with her two daughters. One – fair, quiet and gentle – was named Snow White after the white roses in their small garden. The other, dark haired, lively, loving to 'skip and dance', was named Rose Red after the red roses. They each wore a rose in their hair – one red, one white – and walked everywhere together holding hands. Then, one cold winter's night, a black bear knocked at their door, making their pet lamb bleat; their dove smashed himself against the windows with fear. The bear's fur was bright with ice. 'I have not come to hurt you,' he said in a deep, soft voice. He called them 'dear children'. They warmed him by the fire, and gently swept the snow from his coat.

Perhaps it was because I was fair, quiet and gentle, my sister dark and lively, that I was enchanted by that fairy tale. It is tale 161 in the Brothers Grimm's two-volume collection of German stories, *Children's and Household Tales* (1812–15), but I knew it in the Ladybird 'Well-Loved Tales' Reading Series 606D, retold by Vera Southgate and illustrated by Eric Winter. It seemed more mysterious and uncanny, somehow, than the other stories in the series. Even the ending is strange, when the dwarf is defeated and the bear becomes a prince. The two sisters, it was clear to me, are both in love with him, but Rose Red is palmed off on a faceless 'brother'. (I wonder if that bear knocking on the door, those girls stroking his fur, influenced *The Tiger Who Came to Tea*?)

The Ladybird imprint was begun by Henry Wills and William Hepworth in 1915, with *Hans Andersen's Fairy Tales*. It was intended to produce 'wholesome and healthy literature for children'. The iconic mini-hardback format we associate with the brand, with 56 pages, roughly 4½" x 7", first appeared in 1940 (*Bunnikin's Picnic Party*, which naturally included more of those anthropomorphic rabbits). It was a response to wartime restrictions on paper supply, with the format chosen because it allowed an entire book to be printed on one large standard sheet of paper – a quad crown, 40" x 30" – then folded and cut to size without any waste. It was economical, enabling the books to retail at a low price which was, for almost thirty years, 2/6d. The distinct aesthetic was also created by a decision not to use children's illustrators but, instead, established commercial artists. While Ladybird soon became famous for non-fiction and nature titles, it was the 'Well-Loved Tales', designed for easy reading, that my generation learnt, stumblingly, to read from. Look and say: 'Once upon a time . . .' Now every picture book section is overrun with retellings of *Cinderella* and *The Three Billy Goats Gruff* – pop-up, flap, rhyming, board, textured, modernized, glittering, with sound effects. But for me fairy tales and Ladybirds were synonymous.

My sister's favourite Ladybird book was a different 'Well-Loved Tale' – another deriving from the Brothers Grimm's collection, *The Elves and the Shoemaker*, also retold by Vera Southgate, with illustrations by Robert Lumley. She was delighted by the shoes the elves helped make, with their bright leathers – blue, red, yellow, green; the pink, fringed ankle boots – and charmed by the miniaturization: the tiny outfits the shoemaker and his wife stitch for the elves, to say thank you; the absurd stockings laid out next to thimble-sized boots and hats with red feathers. It is a story in which immense powers are used to achieve small domestic goals, making me think of Angela Carter's lovely summation: 'A fairy tale is a story in which one king goes to another king to borrow a cup of sugar.'

Marina Warner, in her short history of the fairy tale *Once Upon a Time*, notes that another term for a fairy tale is a 'wonder tale', from the German *Wundermärchen*. The supernatural is another defining characteristic of these stories, an implicit or explicit sense of magic. For a child, to whom life itself is a wonder, the tales reflect their sense of the world's still-endless possibilities. G. K. Chesterton has written beautifully in his essay 'The Ethics of Elfland':

> The only words that ever satisfied me as describing Nature are the terms used in the fairy books, 'charm', 'spell', 'enchantment'. They express the arbitrariness of the fact and its mystery. A tree grows fruit because it is

a *magic* tree. Water runs downhill because it is bewitched. The sun shines because it is bewitched.

However, it should also be noted that fairy tales were not always considered children's literature. The term 'fairy tale' ('conte de fées') was first used by Madame d'Aulnoy in the seventeenth century, when such stories circulated amongst intellectuals in the salons of Paris, often disguising critiques of court. Her contemporary Charles Perrault, writer of such famous tales as 'Cinderella', 'The Sleeping Beauty', 'Puss in Boots' and 'Bluebeard', also attended these salons, and the morals they extract are clearly aimed at a sophisticated adult audience rather than a four-year-old. 'Little Red Riding Hood', for example, ends (in Angela Carter's translation) with the insight that: 'There are real wolves, with hairy pelts and enormous teeth; but also wolves who seem perfectly charming, sweet-natured and obliging, who pursue young girls in the street and pay them the most flattering attentions.'

It was the Victorians, Marina Warner notes, who 'nudged the material into the nursery'. In 1823 when the Grimms' *Children's and Household Tales* were first published in England in translation, the caricaturist George Cruikshank's frontispiece showed a laughing grandad and a granny reading to little ones. His other pictures conjured, in Warner's words: 'sweet-faced heroines, plucky lads and dancing elves. The magical animals are comical and endearing, the giants are goofy, their rage is absurd and easily managed.' The lightness was teased out; the darker shadows ignored. They were illustrations to bait the children and soothe their parents, beginning the process of turning fairy tales into picture book fodder.

These tales of bewitchment also suited Victorian nannies as they still asserted a kind of morality – if we pay attention, we notice that magic is always depicted as the consequence of a human action. Chesterton writes:

> For the pleasure of pedantry I will call it the Doctrine of Conditional Joy. Touchstone talked of much virtue in an 'if'; according to elfin ethics all virtue is in an 'if'. The note of the fairy utterance always is, 'You may live in a palace of gold and sapphire, *if* you do not say the word "cow"'; or, 'You may live happily with the King's daughter, *if* you do not show her an onion.' The vision always hangs upon a veto. All the dizzy and colossal things conceded depend upon one small thing withheld.

And what is this if not also a description of the ethics of grown-ups? How rarely, after all, adults really explain to their children why they must or must not do something. Instead, enchantments depend upon routine chores. *If* you eat that cabbage you can have an ice cream. *If* you get in the pram I'll fetch your teddy. *If* you poo in the potty you can have that story you love about Rumpelstiltskin. *If* you go to sleep, the fairy will come and swap your milk tooth for a coin.

My father's favourite story as a child was, by one of those strange coincidences that happen when you are in love, the same as my mother's. It was in a 1950s Collins anthology, *My Book of Elves and Fairies*, and told of Griselda, who, every time she cleaned the windows, found the rain fairies sliding down them in their muddy boots.

He liked to tell me stories about fairies too. When I was small my father told me on a couple of occasions about the Cottingley Fairies. In 1917, in Cottingley in Yorkshire, nine-year-old Frances Griffiths was staying in the home of her cousin, sixteen-year-old Elsie Wright. To their mothers' irritation, they often played together by the beck at the bottom of the garden and came back with sodden feet and clothes. They had to go to the beck though, they explained, in order to visit the fairies. Elsie borrowed her father's camera to take a photograph that would prove it.

When he saw the image of Frances with four dancing

A. ALICE AND THE FAIRIES.
Copyright Photograph taken July, 1917.

fairies, Arthur Wright, a keen amateur photographer who had given his daughter some lessons, dismissed it as a 'prank'. But Elsie's mother, Polly, believed. It was after attending a lecture at the Theosophical Society in Bradford in 1919 on 'Fairy Life' that Polly Wright showed others the photograph, along with another Elsie had taken of a gnome. All things supernatural were in fashion amongst a public exhausted by war and looking for escape. When the photos came to the attention of a leading member of the society, Edward Gardner, he was ecstatic, claiming that: 'the fact that two young girls had not only been able to see fairies, which others had done, but had actually for the first time ever been able to materialize them at a density sufficient for their images to be recorded on a photographic plate, meant that it was possible that the next cycle of evolution was underway.' The two girls spoke to Gardner about how they would '*tice* the fairies, as they called their way of attracting them'. Sir Arthur Conan Doyle – doctor, cricketer, inventor of Sherlock Holmes and keen spiritualist – became involved, asking to print the images alongside an article he was writing for *The Strand Magazine*. More photographs appeared in 1920: 'Frances and the Leaping Fairy', 'Fairy Offering Posy of Harebells to Elsie', 'Fairies and their Sun-Bath'. Doyle wrote a book entitled *The Coming of the Fairies* (1922), in which he claimed: 'To the objections of photographers that the fairy figures show quite different shadows to those of the human our answer is that ectoplasm, as the etheric protoplasm has been named, has a faint luminosity of its own, which would largely modify shadows.' He believed that: 'The recognition of their existence will jolt the material twentieth-century mind out of its heavy ruts in the mud, and will make it admit that there is a glamour and mystery to life.'

I loved this story, so much so that, when I was five, I claimed that I saw a fairy in a bush. I'm fairly sure I made it up, but I wanted it to be true so much, I convinced myself. I can still see my fib so vividly: the little, rustling fairy in the shadows with her dark hair and dress the colour of a blackberry stain. Did I make it up to impress my father; to be like Elsie? Did I need, even then, to escape the muddy rut of the everyday, to believe in mystery?

Even as my father told me the story of the Cottingley Fairies though, I realize now, he must have known they were faked. After all, what could have prompted his telling but the fact that in 1983 the cousins admitted in the magazine *The Unexplained* that the pictures were staged? Elsie confessed that she had copied the pictures from a children's book – a popular illustrated anthology called *Princess Mary's Gift Book*. But my dad let me believe.

Frances said: 'I can't understand to this day why they were taken in – they wanted to be taken in.'

Another influence on my vision was, certainly, the Flower Fairy books written and illustrated by Cicely Mary Barker. The first of these, *Flower Fairies of the Spring* (1923), came out just a year after Doyle's *The Coming of Fairies*, and benefited from the same wave of enthusiasm for 'little people'. In 1983 they too resurfaced in the public's consciousness, when the Hornby Flower Fairy Dolls were released. There was a gift shop in our village called The Bow Window, which had jewellery and wrapping paper, and a children's area upstairs, and I began collecting the reissued Flower Fairy books from there. I remember being bribed with them ('*If* you try and ride your bike without stabilizers, you can have *Flower Fairies of the Summer*'). I remember getting a flower press at the same time and squashing red campion and cowslip; being allowed my own little patch of garden and planting candytuft. For my birthday I asked for the 7″ plastic dolls with stiff floral skirts: Heliotrope, Narcissus, Sweet Pea. We had the petal shower; a secret garden with a swing and a dew-drop pond. *Flower Fairies of the Winter* was published posthumously in 1985, and I raided my (Beatrix Potter) money bank for a copy straight away.

Cicely Mary Barker was the daughter of a seed-merchant who died at forty-three from a virus contracted from contaminated corn. Along with her sister, Dorothy, she had to make her own living, and began to illustrate cards. Barker was largely self-taught – like Edward Lear she suffered from epilepsy which made her an outsider, unable to attend school – although she took correspondence courses and briefly attended the Croydon School of Art. She claimed to draw 'without any real thought or attention to artistic theories', but she was also meticulous, always making careful preparatory sketches of flowers from life, and even obtaining cuttings of less common botanical specimens from Kew Gardens. Barker had her own studio in her garden where she kept a trunk of Flower Fairy costumes she had made by hand, along with wings assembled from gauze and twigs. As models for her fairies, she used real children from the kindergarten school her sister started. Gladys Tidy, an eight-year-old girl who came to her house every Saturday to do household work like black-leading the stove for a shilling, also posed for Barker. Later Tidy recalled she had to go through the below-stairs back door on Saturdays, but was allowed through the front door when she was the 'Primrose Fairy'.

The tension between accuracy and fantasy, experience and innocence, is the appeal of the pictures, although Barker was scrupulous even in her introductions, telling the readers in the introduction to *Flower Fairies of the Wayside*:

> Let me say quite plainly, that I have drawn all the plants and flowers very carefully, from real ones; and everything I have said about them is as true as I could make it. But I have never seen a fairy; the fairies and all about them are just 'pretend' (it's nice to pretend about fairies).

I, like many children, knew the truth of this last aside, and still get a shiver, as if in the presence of sorcery, to hear 'The Song of the Daisy Fairy':

> Come to me and play with me,
> I'm the babies' flower;
> Make a necklace gay with me,
> Spend the whole long day with me,
> Till the sunset hour.

Anyway, Barker never said fairies *didn't* exist, only that she hadn't seen them, and it was safer (I thought) to bet on their existence, given that, as J. M. Barrie pointed out: 'every time a child says "I don't believe in fairies" there is a fairy somewhere that falls down dead.'

Magic is the refuge of the powerless. The dream that the grim everyday might burst its banks: a bare cooking pot pour out endless porridge; a broom become a means of escape; a wish a weapon.

Girls perhaps most of all have historically felt powerless, and the appeal of magic has been strong. Alison Uttley, in her novel *The Country Child*, evokes a world in which 'Jinny Green-teeth' lives under the green scum of the mill pond and drags down little children; where wishes can be made on oxlips, stars, clover, 'the new moon, white bluebells, the first cuckoo'. Even I, my childhood sunny with second-wave feminism, longed desperately for supernatural power. Just as I hallucinated fairies, so I would stare at the bathroom light bulb until my retinas were spangled in the hope it would turn me into Supergirl; would spend hours making spells: whispering made-up incantations, stirring up a potion of dandelion and stone. I loved all the beginner's modes of prophecy – *he loves me not*, black cats, spat cherry stones: *tinker, tailor, soldier, sailor* . . . I remember, from infants all the way up to high school my friends and I would spend hours trying to regress into past lives (I was always some kind of maudlin Victorian orphan) or levitate.

There is a distinction, though, between the model of

femininity offered by fairies and that offered by witches. The desire for fairies is for a world beneath or within this one. A secret, more beautiful world we might discover in our ordinary domestic lives if we are just attentive enough. It is a world that will be revealed to girls who are heedful and quiet, one that picture books populate with small, delicate, pretty creatures who sip droplets of dew and take very small bites off petal plates. Witches are different. They take domestic items (cooking pots, brooms) and use them to subvert and escape. They cackle, they curse, they make stuff *happen*, they terrify people. I wanted to *see* a fairy, but I wanted to *be* a witch.

I'm not entirely sure why, as the only witch I recall seeing in my preschool years was the rather useless Meg. (This is despite trips every Halloween to nearby Pendle Hill, site of the famous witch-hunt, during which my father would encourage us to spot witches as we drove along.) Meg and Mog and Owl first appeared in *Meg and Mog* in 1972, in the series written by Helen Nicoll. It was illustrated by Jan Pieńkowski who has spoken of his early memories of growing up on a farm in Poland, a 'tiny medieval world' where they raised baby deer and pet fox cubs. The coachman's wife would persuade him to drink his boiled milk by telling him tales about a witch, each of which ended on a cliff-hanger. He has said: 'I used to have terrible dreams, nightmares, of this witch, always chasing me and trying to put me in a pot.' Baba Jaga's house was perched on a chicken's foot.

He was three when Poland was invaded. His family were soon moving around the continent to Austria,

Germany and Italy, before settling in Herefordshire in 1946. In the early seventies, Pieńkowski met Helen Nicoll while they were both working for the BBC. She had an idea about a witch and her cat, and Judith Elliott at Heinemann commissioned two books. As Nicoll lived near Marlborough in Wiltshire and Pieńkowski lived in London, they established the routine of meeting to work at the Membury service station on the M4. (Pieńkowski, in his moving obituary for Nicoll in *The Guardian* in 2012, noted: 'I always brought a little bunch of flowers to put on our table.')

Meg and Mog begins with Meg waking up, getting dressed, stepping on Mog (MEEEOW) and making breakfast in her cauldron, like a spell for stomach ache, out of three eggs, bread, cocoa, milk, jam and a kipper. Pieńkowski's childhood nightmares have been sublimated into a cheerful palette of primary colours, inspired by traditional Polish embroidery. The ordinary routine becomes a zany comic strip. Later, a Halloween ritual goes wrong and she turns her friends Bess, Jess, Tess and Cress into mice. This is typical – Pieńkowski claims that he made one condition at the start of the series that 'if the witch were to make a spell, it must never work' – as is her shrugged response: 'I'll have to change them back, next Halloween.' Witchcraft is a fantasy of power over matter, but Meg's power is completely uncontrollable. It can make *something* happen, but the *what* is almost always a surprise to Meg herself. *Abracadabra* unleashes anarchy, a series of random events during which nothing will be learnt. It is dangerous fun, like a child repeating a swear word – gleefully observing its strange effects without understanding how exactly it works ('I must have put in too much bacon,' she notes in *Meg's Eggs*).

Or perhaps Meg is more like a mother. She tries to provide – food, holidays, a car – but things always go wrong in an onslaught of onomatopoeia (CLANG, CRUNCH, SQUAWK, EEEEE, SPLAT). Her authority, the adult knowledge supposedly contained within her spells, is time after time exposed as negligible, just bluff and error, but her family unit muddle through – a fact that is, in its way, empowering.

I, too, had a magical parent whose powers were unreliable.

Perhaps the time has come to write about my father's psychic abilities, which were a huge part of my childhood. I have held back over many years because I do not want to expose these powers to real, adult scrutiny. I know they cannot have been true, yet I sincerely believe them to be true. I am reminded of a phrase by Emily Dickinson: 'we both believe and disbelieve a hundred times an hour, which keeps believing nimble.' Of course all adults dissemble about magic – about the Sandman and the Easter Bunny and Christ's miracles – but belief, in my home, was a particularly nimble thing. On our bookshelf was a guide to bending spoons; on a clear night my dad would watch out over the reservoir for UFOs.

Where do I begin? Before my dad was born perhaps. He told us that he had somehow retained all the memories of both my Grandad and Granny Pollard up until the moment of his conception. My father was usually boastful in a forgivable, boyish, bursting-with-pride kind of way, but about this supernatural power he was strangely muted. It wasn't pleasant, to know these things: to recall all their small discomforts and sorrows.

When my dad was a child, he heard his father claim that during the war, while posted in India, he had seen a tiger. 'No you didn't,' my dad supposedly said. 'You were too scared, you stayed in the tent.'

In this telling my grandad turned white at his small child's uncanny knowledge.

My dad had other fragments of my grandad's memories from India too: an awkward gay encounter; a visit to a Taj Mahal filthy and stinking with neglect. Of his mother's memories, he only said that he remembered her wedding night. She felt disgusted.

The idea of genetic memory has always seemed to me an argument against having children. How terrifying, to think your sleeping babe has suckled on your darkest thoughts; all that filthy mess you want to protect them from. That they can judge you like God. What better revenge could there be against inadequate parents than knowing who they are? It's the set-up for a horror film.

Were the memories inherited, though? There was a blurry area, because my dad could also read people's minds, although he generally chose not to – he didn't like what he saw. (For example, there was that time, verified by my Uncle John, when he went into a pub and said to a man at the bar, 'You didn't get on with your father, did you?' and the man replied, shaken, 'How did you know?' It later transpired that he had murdered him.)

So many other tales, too, imbued my childhood with a sense of larger powers; unseen forces. My dad had slept in a haunted house riddled with cold spots; encountered a panther in a bush by the reservoir; seen a glimmering aura on my cousin Sally. Once, he constructed a voodoo doll of someone hateful he worked with at school, stuck pins into it in our garage, then stopped (with fear and guilt) when that person was hospitalized. Most commonly, though, there were premonitions. My dad was perpetually getting *feelings* about the future, especially the outcomes of horse races (steeplechase only). Once he *knew* not to drive his car on an icy night, less than twenty-four hours before the brakes failed. When he met my mother at a dance at teacher-training college in Poulton, legend has it he went straight to his friend and said: 'That's the woman I'm going to marry.'

For a while, he hoped I might have psychic abilities too. It was I, not Mary, who was lined up to take after him. There was an occasion when I was about three when I spent all day demanding my Muppet annual. My mum repeatedly told me I didn't have one, until my dad came home from teaching at school brandishing a find from the jumble sale: 'Look what I've got you, Clare – a Muppet annual!' When I finally got to Junior 2 and he was my teacher (I'd call him 'sir' at the dinner table) we did mind-reading in class and I guessed all of his numbers correctly.

But in the end, my intuition failed me. When he first became ill, I was so certain it wasn't cancer. I knew. I had a *feeling*. But it was still cancer.

Now that he's dead, I'll never know for sure how much he believed in his own powers or made them up; what was amusement and what was serious. What really went on in my dad's head? I haven't inherited that knowledge. But although I don't believe him I still believe him. I want to live in the world that he told me I lived in, with its 'glamour and mystery'. I want to be taken in.

Pieńkowski's bold, black line illustrations are memorable for me in a way that only Roger Hargreaves' Mr Men and Little Miss books can parallel. As Charlie Brooker has written in *The Guardian*, 'The way Roger Hargreaves drew a shoe is still the way a shoe looks when I picture it. Same with a house. Or a hat. Or a butcher. Or a wizard. Or a cloud.' The series began in 1971 with *Mr Tickle*, inspired by Hargreaves' son, Adam, asking what a tickle looked like. The answer was round and orange, with very long arms. Hargreaves always wrote stories that would take less than five minutes to read, calling them 'bedtime stories for weary daddies'. He drew in Magic Marker, his strong lines masking the way colour spread across the page in the days before bleed-proof paper. He liked to draw the smiles in last, to bring the characters to life.

The Mr Men books also frequently use fairy tale, magic and myth – Misterland is a world of kings, giants, shrinking spells, wishing wells, goblins, tiny doors in trees, and, frequently, wizards (Adam Hargreaves has noted that when his dad ran out of plot ideas he would always introduce a wizard). Mr Strong, when he fills an upside-down barn with the river to put out a 'blazing cornfield', nods to the Fifth Labour of Hercules: diverted rivers cleaning the Augean Stables. Miss Bossy's relentless magic boots allude to the red-hot iron shoes put on the wicked stepmother at the end of Snow White's wedding or Hans Christian Andersen's monstrous red shoes. There is another way in which they nod to old tales too – in the oral markers which draw attention to the teller. As Philip Pullman has noted, 'a fairy tale is not a text', it should have a living connection to voice, and the Mr Men books frequently break the fourth wall and draw attention to the listener, still up in bed. Questions are asked ('Can you giggle and eat cornflakes at the same time?'); gossipy advice is given. Mr Tickle's hand is perhaps 'already creeping to the door of this room'. Hargreaves even appears in *Mr Small* and *Little Miss Star*, in the kind of metatextual gesture that seemed so fresh and bold to me as a child that it primed me to get excited about Martin Amis years later.

Certain things still seem to me to be delightful about the Mr Men and Little Miss books. The meals, for example, whether scaled to bizarrely differing appetites (sixty-six sausages vs half a pea, one crumb and a drop of lemonade), or just ridiculous ('a nice hot cup of cake'). The practical jokes (toothpaste in a cake! A bedful of jam!). The sheer number of lands too, each with its own strange laws – Loudland where mice roar; Happyland where daisies grin; Miseryland where the birds wake up and weep; Muddleland where worms live in trees; Nonsenseland, with its blue grass and pink trees and yellow snow. Fatland, Cleverland, Sleepyland, Coldland. Like the fifty-five fictitious cities described by Marco Polo in Italo Calvino's *Invisible Cities* (published in 1972, just a year after the first Mr Men book, *Mr Tickle*) which each say something about Venice, every time Hargreaves describes a land he is saying something about human nature.

But perhaps we should look a little closer at what Hargreaves is actually saying. I have read the entire Mr Men and Little Miss box sets, in order, so that you don't have to, and the effect is similar to the time I read the King James Bible in order – you realize there is actually no coherent moral system there at all. The hierarchy of sins is utterly random. Wondering what's happening behind a wall is punishable (*Mr Nosey*) but physical contact without consent (tickling random strangers, hugging people who don't want to be hugged) is apparently fine (*Mr Tickle*, *Little Miss Hug*). Being slow or lazy evokes sympathy but Mr Greedy is force-fed sausages the size of pillows until he feels ill, like a child with a bullying father. Wanting to be a star is acceptable, but the clever or talkative need humiliating. Saving money is reprehensible, you have to spend your money on repairing your roof and buying pictures for your walls (*Mr Mean*). On the other hand, when Mr Tall leaves Mr Small at the beach and it takes him a year to walk back, this is hilarious.

Magic in these books is used for instrumental, punitive means, to reduce and not expand. An eye for an eye, aka a 'taste of your own medicine', is frequently dispensed. In Charlie Brooker's neat precis:

> In each story Mr Titular wakes up, has breakfast (usually eggs, consumed in a manner that vividly illustrates his character), goes for a walk, encounters a worm or a wizard or a shopkeeper, learns a harsh moral lesson and then crawls home, a changed man, hopelessly broken by experience.

In making his characters personifications of abstract nouns, Hargreaves is drawing on the tradition of the medieval morality play in which Everyman would meet Strength, Justice, Sloth and Pity. Virtue becomes *Mr Good*, Gluttony turns into *Mr Greedy*. But these qualities are then judged in the absence of God: there is no heaven to aspire to, only acceptance within the Misterland community. An Amazon reviewer of *Mr Messy*, Hamilton Richardson, wrote rather wonderfully:

> If *Nineteen Eighty-Four* or *The Trial* had been a children's book, *Mr Messy* would be it. No literary character has ever been so fully and categorically obliterated by the forces of social control. Hargreaves may well pay homage to Kafka and Orwell in his work, but he also goes well beyond them.

Mr Neat and Mr Tidy march into his home against his protestations and make everything neat 'as a pin', a suitably painful image. Then they forcibly bathe him (grabbing one arm each) and transform him into a faceless pink blob, the basis of Mr Messy's entire identity erased – something that happens repeatedly in these books, always leaving Hargreaves with the uncomfortable problem of what to call his characters in the final pages. In story after story, they are normalized into namelessness.

Elsewhere, physical violence is a perfectly acceptable way to coerce characters into obedience – Mr Nosey is set upon with a hammer; Miss Naughty has her nose tweaked raw; Little Miss Trouble is ticklebumped into submission (we are reminded that the UK did not ban corporal punishment in schools until 1986, and it is still legal to smack your child). As commenters have also noted, there is something incredibly sexist about the whole set-up. The Mr Men live in an almost entirely women-free world, while the 'Little' of Little Miss is instantly diminishing, and they are pointedly not Mrs Women. Incredibly, the first Little Miss was *Little Miss Bossy* (1981), her style of hat marking her out as a middle-aged spinster, in which we witness the unedifying spectacle of several Mr Men combining forces to punish her (she has the temerity to call out Mr Nosey's nosiness and Mr Noisy's noisiness). Soon all the stereotypes were being wheeled out, including Little Scatterbrain, Dotty, Contrary, Chatterbox and Plump(!!), who was only changed to *Little Miss Greedy* in 1988.

Roger Hargreaves had a stroke while walking down to breakfast and died aged just fifty-two. His 24-year-old son Adam, who later took over the brand, has carried on inventing new Mr Men and Little Misses ever since, though still signing the covers with his father's signature.

The franchise has been a magic porridge pot, churning out a never-ending slurry of profits and new titles. *Little Miss Hug*, *Little Miss Fabulous*, *Little Miss Sparkle*, *Little Miss Princess* (what an ugly little run of stereotypes that is). They have licensed a Mr Glug to peddle Evian Water, a Mr First to advertise the money transfer company World First. In 2004, Hargreaves' widow, Christine, sold the rights to UK entertainment group Chorion for £28 million. After it was forced into administration, in 2011, Sanrio, creators of Miffy's nemesis Hello Kitty, acquired the rights. There are Mr Cool toilet seat covers; Little Miss Helpful's Gel Packs; Mr Funny's Runny Honey; Little Miss Naughty Underwear in La Senza. There are even adult titles, following the success of the jocular adult Ladybirds (*The Ladybird Book of the Mid-Life Crisis* etc., etc.). You can buy *Mr Greedy Eats Clean to Get Lean*; *Little Miss Busy Surviving Motherhood*; *Mr Messy's Guide to Student Life*; *Mr Tickle's Guide to Women* [sic]. The Mr Men and Little Miss Libraries account for over 100 million book sales and are the second-biggest children's books of all time after Harry Potter, but sometimes I think a wizard needs to make it stop.

Fairy tales were probably first told by women. The female storyteller is there in the figure of Old Mother Goose. The Grimm Brothers gathered over twenty stories from a group of educated young women in Kassel who would meet and recite tales they had heard from nannies or servants. Another forty came from Dorothea Viehmann, a poor tailor's wife and mother of six who would go to their house on market days once she had sold her vegetables.

Talking about fairy tales often seems to mean talking about femininity. So many of the stories have female protagonists who display kindness and courage, but they are also filled with darker versions of womanhood such as witches and crones. In the early 1812 editions of 'Little Snow White' and 'Hansel and Gretel' the wicked stepmothers are actually biological mothers – they were only changed to stepmothers by the Brothers Grimm in 1819. Queens, sacrificial or self-regarding, die in childbirth; drip blood on to snow; rage at their reflections; utter curses. Time destroys or corrupts feminine power. Women my age are feared or disappeared.

The younger women in fairy tales are, of course, mainly princesses or princesses-in-waiting, their female attributes still fresh and so delightful. I prefer the ones who don't know they are princesses yet, but whose nobility is recognized through their gentleness and sacrifice, because at least then the palace and tiara seem earned. (The first play I 'wrote', aged four, inspired by my mother's play scripts for the WI, was about 'The Little Goose Girl'.) But to be honest, as a child I don't really recall princesses being a *thing*. Now, the sin of vanity is apparently no longer a *thing*. Search children's books for 'princess' on Amazon and you get over 10,000 results, with most of these princess-protagonists glittery from the start, and many titles churned out to meet a seemingly insatiable desire for sparkles. (A low point is perhaps the uber-objectifying book *That's Not My Princess*, from the

That's Not My . . . franchise by Fiona Watt and Rachel Wells, in which the speaker realizes it isn't their princess because 'her fan is too fluffy'.)

As books have become increasingly gendered, so the princess, born into beauty and bling, has come to predominate in publishing for little girls. And as those little girls have grown up into millennials, princess-culture has spread: unicorn lattes and pool-floats, rainbow layer cake, #princessnails. The aesthetic of Instagram, with its preening selfies, is the aesthetic of princesses. Mirror, mirror.

Such is the ubiquity of the princess picture book genre now that it can accommodate a whole sub-genre – princesses who defy princess stereotypes – in titles such as *The Strong Princess*; *The Wrestling Princess*; *Beware, Princess!*; *The Princess in Black*; *Dangerously Ever After*; *Don't Kiss the Frog!*; *The Worst Princess*. These are books whose intention, like Disney's recent *Brave* or *Frozen*, seems to be to lure in princess-mad little girls, and then expose them to a more feminist storyline. The question has to be whether, however progressive the narrative, ceding to the same type of privileged protagonist yet again (upper-class, able-bodied, pretty, largely white) undoes this good work, and how radical any book that adds to the ocean of pink can truly be. It is worth looking at some of the alternative-princess books in a little more detail.

My clear favourite is arguably the first – *The Paper Bag Princess* (1980) written by Robert Munsch and illustrated by Michael Martchenko. In it a princess called Elizabeth is in love with a handsome prince called Ronald. But a

dragon kidnaps him and scorches off her clothes (smoke, in the picture, masks most of her nakedness, but she is definitely still a flat-chested young girl). Elizabeth makes herself a dress out of a paper bag and in a marvellous picture is shown tensing all her muscles with fury in a bone-strewn wasteland.

Elizabeth then rescues Ronald, mainly by appealing to the dragon's ego ('I bet you could fly around the world really fast') until the beast is exhausted.

The writer Robert Munsch is an interesting figure, very honest about his addiction and mental health problems, who trained seven years to be a Jesuit priest and worked in an orphanage. He is also the author of one of the most strange, sentimental picture books ever written,

Love You Forever (1986), which he wrote after he and his wife had lost two stillborn children. In it, a mother sings a lullaby to her baby, announcing that she will love her baby forever. Munsch has said it was 'my song to my dead babies'. The mother repeats the song as the son grows up, and he ends up singing it back to his mother on her death bed. As if that wasn't enough to process, the cover also features a little boy sitting by a toilet.

The Paper Bag Princess, though, is the opposite of sentimental. Munsch was working in a childcare centre in Oregon when he first told Elizabeth's story, inspired by his wife, who worked there too (they met 'over a diaper') and who was tired of his usual dragon tales. She asked: 'Why can't the princess save the prince?' It was perhaps Munsch's belief that 'to kids there's only one character in the story and that's themselves' that made him realize this idea could not only be radical but life-changing. In the original ending, Ronald's lack of gratitude when rescued made Elizabeth punch him in the nose, but when Martchenko drew this they decided it looked too violent. In the final version, Elizabeth instead utters those brilliant, defiant lines to Ronald:

Your hair is nice.
You look like a PRINCE.
But you are a BUM.

The word BUM, in this context, read out by an adult at the end of a fairy tale, is still shocking. It makes my children giddy with daring. For a while, in the UK,

Australia and New Zealand, Scholastic decided that people didn't call each other bums and Ronald should be a toad. But even if small children don't quite get the connotations of Ronald being idle and useless (a vagrant, a lounger), the pure delight of being able to (righteously) shout a synonym for bottom is the genius of the book. Toad isn't the same at all.

The classicist Mary Beard has cited it as one of the books that made her a feminist and observed that its last line is: 'power for you, in a nutshell'.

Princess Smartypants (1986), written and illustrated by Babette Cole, was also an early trailblazer in the alternative-princess genre and is great fun. In this story, Princess Smartypants wants to be a Ms not a Mrs, so sets all the princes who come to try and win her hand impossible tasks involving her pet dragons, a frightening forest and polished glass towers. When one suitor, Prince Swashbuckle, finally succeeds in completing her tasks, Princess Smartypants solves the problem by giving him a 'magic kiss' that turns him into a toad. Having frightened off all potential suitors, she then lives happily ever after.

Babette Cole was a provocateur of the picture book world who spoke openly in interviews about her secret love affairs, as well as writing a book about sex being fun and how mummies and daddies 'fit together' – *Mummy Laid an Egg!* (1995) – that tabloid rants branded 'the Kama Sutra for kids aged three'. She viewed *Princess Smartypants* as her 'autobiography'. The pictures are lively and funny – I love the princess's dungarees and roller-disco moves, as well as her beloved pets (a cat, a dog, a pony, various dragons, a hairy spider, a castle-sized snail) that seem to have been loosely based on Cole's own menagerie at her home in Lincolnshire. But *Princess Smartypants*, 'very pretty and rich', whose idea of pleasing herself is eating chocolates, drinking cocktails, painting her nails, sunbathing and doing 'exactly as she pleased', is only feminist in the way, say, *Sex and the City* is feminist.

Zog (2010), writer Julia Donaldson and illustrator Axel Scheffler's more recent attempt at the alternative-princess genre, is a little better in that Princess Pearl has ambitions beyond a life of leisure, but it is still an odd one. The hero of the title, Zog, is a young dragon at dragon school, learning skills such as flying and fire-breathing and constantly having accidents. Miraculously, Princess Pearl always seems to be nearby when these accidents happen and keen to assist. Though it is framed as empowering that Pearl wants to be a doctor, she fits into a feminized, caring role more akin to a nurse – always available to offer Zog a sticking plaster, a peppermint, a *poor you*. When Zog is told that for his next lesson he has to learn how to kidnap a princess, rather than encouraging him to rebel against the entire patriarchal dragon educational system, she offers to let herself be captured. Is it okay because it's tongue-in-cheek, like pole-dancing in the 1990s? At the end the unattractive Sir Gadabout 'the Great', with his awful moustache, tries to rescue her, and whilst she boldly insists she doesn't need rescuing, she still somehow ends up partnering off with him as they agree to embark on a career as medics together and fly off on Zog, who has volunteered to be their ambulance.

We recently borrowed the sequel *Zog and the Flying Doctors* (2016) from the library, and I found it even more confused in its message – Zog is diminished to the status of a clumsy vehicle, basically, whilst Pearl is locked in a tower by a misogynist uncle who asks where her 'pretty, frilly dress' is (although she's not in jeans, by any means, and is already wearing a very feminine dress) and makes her sew 'pretty cushions'. She is reduced to the usual passive-princess position while her drippy partner, Gadabout, somehow gets to be the protagonist: Prince Charmless on a quest to save her by gathering the ingredients needed for a medicine. At the end Pearl cures her uncle and he admits girls can be doctors – but again, the king isn't punished or even challenged. Everyone is just very grateful he's stopped locking women up . . . Feminism, whoop.

Since Cate was born, I often think of that line in F. Scott Fitzgerald's *The Great Gatsby*, when Daisy says, bitterly, of her daughter: 'I hope she'll be a fool—that's the best thing a girl can be in this world, a beautiful little fool.' Too often that seems like the central message of princess culture, but I don't think beauty or stupidity will help Cate in the future that is coming. There are women I know and admire who love costume jewellery and power-ballads, and I've never had a problem with Gruff liking conventional boy-stuff like Transformers or Ninjas, but polyester Disney ballgowns set my teeth on edge. My daughter has not discovered princesses yet, or barely, though last week I discovered her looking in the mirror saying, 'Princess Cate, Princess Cate.' She hasn't got this from me. Is it nursery? A friend? You cannot protect your child completely; there will always be a spindle somewhere to prick her finger.

There is something terrible about the world of princesses – their spellbound servants; their christenings, alarming with gifts. How they're made from a mother's longing. Breathing dressing-up dolls with ruby lips, sapphire eyes, pure gold hair. 'All the dizzy and colossal things' hanging on such genetic fluke. When you have everything already, what storyline exists but one in which disaster befalls you? A woodsman dragging you into the forest; a coma; a poisoned apple? It is like a metaphor for being born into Western privilege, and it makes me feel guilty and fearful.

It also made G. K. Chesterton uneasy. He observes in 'The Ethics of Elfland':

> This princess lives in a glass castle, that princess on a glass hill; this one sees all things in a mirror; they may all live in glass houses if they will not throw stones. For this thin glitter of glass everywhere is the expression of the fact that the happiness is bright but brittle, like the substance most easily smashed by a housemaid or a cat. And this fairy-tale sentiment also sank into me and became my sentiment towards the whole world. I felt

and feel that life itself is as bright as the diamond, but as brittle as the window-pane.

Maybe, though, little girls are not so easily made into fools. When I take Cate to Ten O'Clock Club, I must admit it is often the girls dressed as Elsa from *Frozen* who are driving the plastic digger most competently; who know all the actions for 'The Banana Song'. The phenomenal global success of the Spanish writer María Isabel Sánchez Vegara's *Little People, Big Dreams* series of picture book biographies, featuring women such as Frida Kahlo, Maya Angelou and Josephine Baker, and *Good Night Stories for Rebel Girls* (2017), created by Elena Favilli and Francesca Cavallo, mean alternative role models are now easier to find in bookshops. As long as it isn't the only option, perhaps a shimmery sprinkle of 'happily ever after' is not too damaging.

'Distance is the soul of the beautiful,' the philosopher Simone Weil said. Fairy tales, so far away and long ago from our children, teach them that pleasurable yearning for a beauty which is always out of reach. We can contemplate the beautiful but never truly possess it. Still, it can fill our hearts with joy that such beauty is possible.

And now it's dusk, and our garden is tangled with yellow and pink roses. Our hollyhocks look like they've grown from magic seeds; are turrets climbing up to the clouds. Cate puts a witch's hat over her mess of golden ringlets. She is making a spell from grass and pebbles and washing-up liquid and most likely snot. She decides she needs to add an elephant, and marches back in the house to get one from the toy box, returning to launch it into her cauldron with a splash.

I watch her at a distance, through the dirty kitchen window, with my washing-up bowl of slimy knives. 'Izzy wizzy,' she shouts at me, laughing, waving her spoon like a wand, and I am transformed.

7. Snow Angels

On toys and Christmas Eve

The literary theorist and philosopher Roland Barthes wrote an essay on the subject of 'Toys' in *Mythologies* (1957), about how they are often just shrunken versions of adult things, as if a child was 'nothing but a smaller man, a homunculus to whom must be supplied objects of his own size'. In his brilliant essay (translated here by Annette Lavers) he rails against the miniature weapons, cash-tills and prams that prepare boys for a world of 'war, bureaucracy, ugliness' and little girls to become housewives. Through such objects 'the child can only identify himself as owner, as user, never as creator; he does not invent the world, he uses it: there are, prepared for him, actions without adventure, without wonder, without joy.' What can children do with a toy iron apart from pretend to iron for a bit and then get bored? What can they do with a toy TV controller apart from mimic their mother, and then, when they realize it doesn't control the TV, cast it aside? These objects have a dual function for capitalism, both inducting children into accepting the norms of adult life, and creating a desire for the next, more stimulating object.

These days all toys, pretty much, annoy me with their

specificity. Give a child a generic ship and all sorts of scenarios are possible: perhaps they will catch fish for their barbecue, find treasure, land on dinosaur island. Perhaps they're violent thieves or running a monkey-rescue boat. Give your kids an *Octonauts* GUP-D and they're either Captain Barnacles saving a manta ray with a net or it's being bagged up for the charity shop. The child is just the owner of a desirable chunk of franchise; an imaginative ready-meal. Free story with every box!

Children still invent when they're given room, though, with sticks and sheets and cardboard. Soft toys, or at least the ones that are like Dogger rather than one of the pups from *PAW Patrol*, can leave a space for creativity. I like the toys that require the invention of a personality, a relationship, a name ('No, Cate, you cannot call the puffin Puffin'). Toys that require the child to become a god-like creator, breathing life into the clay or 100 per cent polyester hollow fibre stuffing.

There is a particular type of magic that features more than any other in children's books – making the inanimate animate. Child development pioneer Jean Piaget's theories suggest that many three- or four-year-olds operate on the simple cognitive schema that things that move are living, so believe that many objects like the sun, clouds and cars are alive. What it means to be 'living', to be 'real', is still not fully grasped. Children have historically been encouraged to act out 'pretend' tea parties and battles with their toys and, as Freud notes in his essay 'The Uncanny', 'are especially fond of treating their dolls like live people', so it is unsurprising that the concepts of aliveness and reality are often explored in children's culture through such toys, from Carlo Collodi's *Pinocchio* (1883), the wooden puppet who wants to be a 'real boy', to Pixar's *Toy Story* franchise.

The Adventure of Two Dutch Dolls and a 'Golliwogg' (1895), written by Bertha Upton and illustrated by Florence K. Upton, an American mother and daughter, is a typical nineteenth-century example, featuring toys rising from their 'wooden sleep' and having an adventure. This example is particularly interesting, though, in that it is argued it constitutes the invention of the golliwog. Florence invented the name for a character based on a minstrel doll found in her aunt's attic, wearing minstrel attire of a bow tie and tails. The huge popularity of the books in Britain and Europe (they wrote thirteen) made the toys a phenomenon, although her failure to trademark the golliwog meant they were soon being used to sell everything from marmalade to aniseed chews. Although he quickly becomes a 'friend' in the original story, there is a definite racism to the 'penny wooden' dolls' first encounter with the golliwog, as they scream at the 'horrid sight' of the 'blackest gnome'. Florence K. Upton later seems to have partly repented after 'wog' became a racist insult, claiming: 'I am frightened when I read the fearsome etymology some deep, dark minds can see in his name.'

After some time spent, rather bizarrely, at Chequers, the official residence of the British Prime Minister, that first golliwog now resides in London, in the V&A Museum of Childhood. You can visit him and see that leather face, the hair made of animal fur, the red lips shut in a quiet smile. The Dutch dolls crowd around him, hands on hips or arms folded; their faces cold and pinched.

So many years later, our culture is still tainted by the uneasy legacy of Florence K. Upton's books. A photograph from 1979 in which I am smiling, surrounded by my teddies and white toy rabbits, shows that I had a golliwog of my own.

More recently, I have been in many shops in Yorkshire that still sell them. Sentimental for the idyll of childhood, we maintain the myth of its utter innocence. We wilfully forget that though babies may be ignorant,

there are always adults consciously manufacturing objects, fears and desires. Pulling the strings.

Perhaps one of the twentieth-century illustrators most associated with living toys is William Nicholson, an illustrator and theatre designer who made the sets for the first dramatization of *Peter Pan* for J. M. Barrie. He had a dramatic family life. After eloping with his wife Mabel in 1893, they had four children, one of whom became the famous painter Ben Nicholson, while another married the poet Robert Graves. Christopher was an architect and Anthony died in France of wounds during the First World War. Mabel herself died in 1918 of the Spanish Flu epidemic. William Nicholson's housekeeper, Adèle Marie Schwarz, was for many years also his mistress.

His masterpiece was *Clever Bill* (1926), which Maurice Sendak called 'among the few perfect picture books for children' and Shirley Hughes has praised as a neglected classic. In *Clever Bill* the postman brings Mary a letter, asking her if she would like to visit her aunt. In her rush to pack she forgets her toy soldier, clever Bill Davis, who sets off in pursuit. There are few words, yet there is an amazing ratcheting up of anticipation and tension – some of the pages simply have the word 'and!!' on them. It is like the dash to the airport at the end of a rom-com.

In *The Velveteen Rabbit* (1922) by Margery Williams, which William Nicholson also illustrated, the Skin Horse famously explains to the Velveteen Rabbit how 'Nursery magic' works. 'Real isn't how you are made,' but rather: 'It's a thing that happens to you. When a child loves you for a long, long time, not just to play with, but REALLY loves you, then you become Real.' It's the same message repeated in the *Toy Story* movies. In such a system, a lonely or isolated individual cannot be real. Realness is something conferred by others, that can only arise through relationships. (Did Nicholson's attentions make Adèle Marie Schwarz feel 'real'?)

In the same year as *Clever Bill*, the writer A. A. Milne and illustrator E. H. Shepard released *Winnie-the-Pooh* (1926), about the toys of Milne's son, Christopher Robin. The original stuffed Winnie-the-Pooh, Piglet, Eeyore, Kanga and Tigger are now on display in the New York public library. Our first glimpse of Winnie-the-Pooh is of him being dragged carelessly down the stairs: 'bump, bump, bump, on the back of his head'. In his ownership of the others, Christopher Robin is treated as a kind of Adam, masterful and benign – 'more like a kindly uncle than a child', Frank Cottrell Boyce has noted.

Numerous accounts have already been written of A. A. Milne and his son Christopher Robin, who found his starring role in the books a burden, saying: 'it seemed to me, almost, that my father had got to where he was by climbing upon my infant shoulders, that he had filched from me my good name and had left me with nothing but the empty fame of being his son.' As a small boy Christopher Robin was photographed in smocks and with his toys, interviewed, encouraged to star in a Pooh pageant in Ashdown Forest as himself and to make a novelty record of Milne's poems set to music called *The Hums of Pooh*. He was also, inevitably, later bullied remorselessly at school, with other boys playing the record over and over. Like Alastair or 'Mouse', the son of Kenneth Grahame (*The Wind in the Willows*), who lay down on a railway track and killed himself, or John Uttley, who only survived his mother Alison Uttley's death by two years before he drove his car off a cliff, Christopher Robin will always be remembered as one of the children somehow sacrificed to children's literature, the books supposedly written for them taking precedence in their parents' lives. Christopher Robin's real life was stolen and made unreal.

Winnie-the-Pooh has one or two pictures on every spread, often inserted into the text in interesting, integral ways. E. H. Shepard's landscapes were directly inspired by Ashdown Forest, where Christopher used to play – its bracken, gorse, pines and silver birches – and the toys often look slightly battered, giving a pleasing texture of reality that grounds Milne's whimsy. The book also seems to belong in the nursery (my copy is inscribed 'Love to our darling Clare on her first Christmas'). Yet the text to image ratio is too heavy, really, for it to satisfy as a picture book. Even reading it now, to my five-year-old, I find myself having to do spontaneous heavy abridgement, skimming over whole conversations and (especially) Pooh's twee songs just to keep the plot moving.

My father loved Winnie-the-Pooh in his own childhood, and Edgworth's village wood became our own Hundred Acre Wood, with our den and muddy patch and expeditions, the Pooh-sticks Bridge, the place we saw Owl, the tracks we would make in the snow. But I think I was probably fonder, like many children, of my father's fondness of the books than the books themselves, and rereading them I often think of Dorothy Parker's acid review of *The House at Pooh Corner* (1928) in *The New Yorker*. (After quoting Pooh's hum 'The more it / SNOWS-tiddely-pom', she notes: 'In fact, so Good a Hum did it seem that he and Piglet started right out through the snow to Hum It Hopefully to Eeyore. Oh darn—there I've gone and given away the plot. I could bite my tongue out.')

By the time I was a child, there was also the flood of Disney tie-ins. At Christmas, I would usually get something with Pooh on it, while my sister got something featuring Piglet. I think I took this as confirmation that she was cuter than me, and vaguely resented being equated with that greedy, tubby, silly blond bear with his icky name. In fairness, though, it seems that 'poo' wasn't used to mean faeces until the 1930s, and 'pooh' is meant in the sense of an exclamation used to express irritation or disgust (the dictionary gives the example 'Oh pooh! Don't be such a spoilsport!'), used perhaps (there are various accounts) because Pooh was always blowing flies off his nose.

Winnie seems to have come from a female bear at London Zoo. Milne recounts that on first hearing the name Winnie-the-Pooh he said, 'But I thought he was a boy?' and Christopher Robin replied, 'He's Winnie-ther-Pooh. Don't you know what "ther" means?' Milne's account is jocular about how this is 'all the explanation you are going to get'. It seems a good explanation to me, though. 'Ther' was clearly not meant as a determiner at all, but a masculine name ending – as adding '-ella' to Nigel makes the girl's name Nigella, so Christopher thought adding his own '-pher' to Winnie would make Winnipher, a boy's name.

It was really Winnipher Pooh.

Enid Blyton, who interviewed A. A. Milne and Christopher Robin for *Teacher's World* early in her career, also famously brought toys to life in her stories for the smallest children, particularly those about Toyland. Blyton was born in 1897 in East Dulwich, South London, on Lordship Lane (I regularly pass her blue plaque above the Builder's Merchants). A phenomenon who produced a disturbing number of titles (at some points averaging 50 a year, and probably publishing somewhere between 600 and 700 altogether – even she lost track), Blyton told psychologist Peter McKellar:

> I shut my eyes for a few minutes, with my portable typewriter on my knee – I make my mind a blank and wait ... The first sentence comes straight into my mind, I don't have to think of it – I don't have to think of anything.

She always wrote after breakfast with her Moroccan red shawl nearby, tapping into her 'undermind', producing up to 10,000 words of this writing a day, like a computer running a program to generate prose. Clearly a workaholic, she wrote the ENTIRE contents of her regular magazine, *Sunny Stories for Little Folks*. Her famous signature soon commanded brand loyalty; by 1958, there were 52 separate companies dealing with her non-book merchandising. Blyton was so dominant in the market that she seems to have stirred particular animosity in her peers. Kathleen Hale was first inspired to create her beloved books about *Orlando the Marmalade Cat* out of sheer loathing for Blyton, whom she nicknamed 'the Pied Blighter'. Blyton's neighbour Alison Uttley, ever malicious, called her a 'vulgar, curled woman'.

Blyton's own life also became, in a way, part of the brand – in an early article she declared: 'I love pretending myself.' Blyton conjured an idyllic homelife, writing in *The Story of My Life*: 'we are a happy little family . . . How could I write good books for children if I didn't care about my own? You wouldn't like my books, if I were that kind of mother!' Yet the memoir fails to mention her affair and subsequent divorce (and the fact she denied her first husband access to his children) and was in many ways just another work of fiction. In *A Childhood at Green Hedges* (1989), her daughter Imogen recalls Blyton as 'without a trace of maternal instinct', having small fans round for games and afternoon tea but mainly ignoring her own children. Most upsettingly, Imogen only remembers her mother reading her a story on a single occasion.

It has been noted that when Blyton discusses ambition in *The Story of My Life*, the words she quotes – without acknowledging the source – belong to Lady Macbeth, the ultimate embodiment of maternal ambivalence.

We fail!
But screw your courage to the sticking place,
And we'll not fail!
[Exclamation marks Blyton's own]

Blyton is mainly remembered now for her work for slightly older children: *The Famous Five, Malory Towers*. Her Mary Mouse books (1942–64), largely illustrated by Olive F. Openshaw, are out of print, though they were once popular enough to merit her churning out twenty-three titles in the series. They tell how, exiled from her mousehole for being too tidy, Mary Mouse becomes a maid at a doll's house, working for Daddy Doll, an ex-sailor doll with a blond moustache, and Mummy Doll who 'needs to rest a lot' because 'the children make her very tired'. It is notable that the animal is subordinate to the humanoid; the born subordinate to the modelled – Blyton again privileging fantasy over reality. With their unusual format, 15 x 7 cms softback pictorial, and limited colours, they have become highly collectable.

Then, of course, there are the Noddy books (1949–63) illustrated by the Dutch artist Harmsen van der Beek (or simply 'Beek'). They came from the conscious intention to create a Disney-style focus character – a European competitor to Mickey Mouse. The idea was conceived by one of Blyton's publishers, Sampson Low, Marston and Company, who in 1949 arranged a meeting between Blyton and Beek. Although they had to use an interpreter, he sketched Toyland, and after what sounds, by her standards, a relaxed four days, Blyton sent over the text of the first two books. Soon a 'Noddy Licensing Co.' had been set up to deal with the merchandising.

Noddy – like Pinocchio – is crafted by a woodcarver but flees in fear when a wooden lion is made, and is befriended by a Brownie, Big Ears. Taken to Toyland, where the houses are built from colourful building blocks, he has to undergo a trial to prove he is a 'real' toy. Later he becomes a taxi driver for the other toys, driving a car with a horn that goes 'parp parp': there is Mr Wobblyman, one of those dolls that can't lie down (basically a Weeble), a skittle family, a clockwork clown. There are also golliwogs. Even those who insist Upton's books are innocent fun find it hard to defend *Here Comes Noddy Again* (1951), where the golliwogs basically car-jack Noddy in the dark, dark wood ('Three black faces suddenly appeared in the light of the car's lamps') and strip him. It has been noted, though, that Toyland is rife with criminals of all types. The academic David Rudd has argued in his fascinating study *Enid Blyton and the Mystery of Children's Literature* that, in many ways, the books themselves are about consumerism: from the bookplates at the start that stress ownership, to the characters' perpetual concern with money, property and theft. It makes sense – as a society we have always used toys to teach children about ownership: wanting and having. There is even one disturbing book in which, Rudd notes, Father Christmas visits Toyland 'like some turkey-farmer examining his seasonal stock'.

*

As an adult, it's hard not to find some of these living toys uncanny, as Freud explored in his essay unpacking E. T. A. Hoffmann's short story 'The Sandman' (1817), with its lifelike doll, Olympia. It is the uncertainty as to whether she is real or not, subject or object, that makes her creepy, like waxworks or puppets or epileptic seizures which 'excite in the spectator the feeling that automatic, mechanical processes are at work'. These things are familiar yet not – *unheimlich*, or unhomely. In Freud's view the uncanny is also related to the return of repressed infantile material.

As children, we create doppelgängers through self-love to ensure our immortality. Our dolls are our other selves; the 'living doll' not an object of fear but of desire. As grown-ups, though, we find the return of these doubles dreadful. In *The Country Child*, Uttley has a chapter in which Susan, getting older, suddenly sees in her doll, Rose, an 'idol' who looks out 'pitifully with her blind all-seeing eyes'. She strips the doll and tries to drown her in the water troughs but, being wooden, 'Like a live thing Rose sprang up and lay floating, a brown Ophelia among the oval damson leaves.' There is something about the way our childish longings won't be suppressed that is profoundly disturbing. When we try to bury them, they bob back up.

Now the boundaries between toys and living beings are blurring, our childhood wishes becoming adult realities. We read in the news about Hello Barbie, with its 8,000 pre-programmed lines of chat that respond to their playmate's vocabulary choices (*You said you wanted to be a veterinarian when you grow up; why don't we talk about animals!),* and stores a record of all its conversations with a child for up to two years. The pink Furby with an unsecured microphone that a stranger within 100 feet can speak through. The My Friend Cayla doll with waist-length golden hair, that collects audio files of the child's voice, name, location and IP address, and that *The Mirror* hacked so it could quote Hannibal Lecter and *Fifty Shades of Grey.*

For how long will picture books about living toys, that explore the boundaries between fantasy and reality, even make sense to our children? In our increasingly atomized society, it sometimes feels as though reality is draining from all of us. We're simulacra of ourselves, posing on Facebook for bots, lacking the relationships that solidify our sense of self. Or is social media making us more real – multiplied into immortality; ♥ed and liked into existence by thousands of followers? Will AI become real when it is loved? What is 'real' anyway?

Perhaps children can ask Alexa in their bedrooms, before she reads their bedtime stories and switches off the light.

Christmas is something that many of these books about toys have in common. It is depicted as a period when toys come to life. Christmas is, after all, when the impossible becomes possible. A time of miracles – visits from angels; the star above a stable; God as a tiny human. I am always moved by Thomas Hardy's poem 'The Oxen' (1915) about the belief that at midnight on Christmas Eve the animals kneel.

So fair a fancy few would weave
In these years! Yet, I feel,
If someone said on Christmas Eve,
'Come; see the oxen kneel,

'In the lonely barton by yonder coomb
Our childhood used to know,'
I should go with him in the gloom,
Hoping it might be so.

A similar concept – that animals can talk on Christmas Eve – is present in Beatrix Potter's *The Tailor of Gloucester*. Many picture books also use this idea of Christmas as a time of miracles reliant on a child's belief, as in Chris Van Allsburg's *The Polar Express* (1985), where a boy is given one of Santa's sleigh bells and tells us: 'At one time, most of my friends could hear the bell, but as years passed, it fell silent for all of them.' It only rings for those who 'truly believe'.

For a child too, toys and Christmas are virtually synonymous. When I think of Christmas I think of agonizing over The List. Skipping around the coffee table until I got dizzy, singing: 'It's the Eve of Christmas Eve.' I'd wake in absolute dark to feel for my grandad's football sock at the end of the bed, bumpy with chocolate money and geegaws; a smooth red apple in the toe. Wait outside the lounge while my dad in his striped pyjamas – dark hair crazed by sleep, blue eyes bleary with a hangover – 'checked' that Father Christmas had visited. 'He's been!!' my dad would exclaim, and we'd rush in giddy with our luck to see treasures heaped in the shadows: a Wonder

Woman costume, annuals, selection boxes, a rocking horse, an erected wigwam that made my sister shout, 'Yay we've got a triangle!!' We opened our presents while Mum fried bacon for sandwiches.

The poet Dylan Thomas, in *A Child's Christmas in Wales* (which I have as a picture book, illustrated by the gifted Edward Ardizzone), has a wonderful passage in which he distinguishes between 'Useful Presents' from aunts – mittens, vests and 'pictureless books in which small boys, though warned with quotations not to, would skate on Farmer Giles' pond and did and drowned; and books which told me everything about the wasp, except why' – and the marvellously 'Useless Presents', including jelly babies, false noses, mewing ducks and painting books in which he could paint the sheep 'sky-blue'. In his memoir *The Bucket*, Allan Ahlberg writes beautifully too about the pillowcase he would find filled on Christmas morning, and how his abiding memory is not the opening but the anticipation: 'that first glimpse on the landing, the mysterious shape, and all my little heart and soul swept up, consumed, in the discovery of it'.

Such is the power of children's desire that it becomes a kind of conjuring, an animating force, in many tales of Christmas Eve. *The Velveteen Rabbit* is first discovered in a stocking with 'nuts and oranges and a toy engine, and chocolate almonds and a clockwork mouse'. The story of the Dutch dolls takes place 'on a frosty Christmas Eve', with 'Peggy Deutschland' telling the other doll:

Get up! get up, dear Sarah Jane!
Now strikes the midnight hour,
When dolls and toys
Taste human joys,
And revel in their power.

E. T. A. Hoffmann also wrote 'The Nutcracker and the Mouse King' (1816), a story in which, in a weird blurring of belief systems, Christmas presents are delivered by the Christ Child flying on 'glowing clouds'. On Christmas Eve a girl called Marie sees toys come to life and do battle with mice. After she has sacrificed many of her presents to protect him, the Nutcracker leads Marie through the door of a closet into another realm: the tinsel and sparkle of 'Christmas Wood', the Marzipan Castle. They become engaged, before Marie leaves the ordinary world forever, abandoning reality for the 'Kingdom of the Dolls'. It has become the basis of Tchaikovsky's famous ballet *The Nutcracker* and is often retold in picture book form – the version I own is translated by Ralph Manheim and illustrated by Maurice Sendak after he made sets for the ballet.

And who can forget another festive story in which a child's playmate becomes animate? On the 26th of December 1982, when I was four, Raymond Briggs' *The Snowman* was first shown on Channel 4. In fact, *The Snowman* (1978) wasn't specifically intended to be a Christmas book. Although it is full of wintry magic, there is no tree or tinsel in the boy's house. But the television adaptation chose to add a cameo from Father Christmas, perhaps inspired by Briggs' 1973 book of the same name. Now no Christmas seems complete without that satsumá nose and those coal eyes being pressed into snow. That strange, muted light of the pencil crayon drawings; the moment where the snowman tips his hat.

I like no sound better than the hush of falling snow.

My father was romantic (in the *true* sense, my mother always says) about the rituals and rhythms of the year, and I am too. Pantomimes, tulips, April Fool's jokes, felt-tipped eggs, the *pock* of tennis balls at Wimbledon, lollies, sniffing roses, *Punch and Judy*, new pencil cases, rain on the roof, conkers, fireworks, treacle toffee. I love that the circus comes once a year to Peckham Common. Like my dad, I am particularly romantic about Christmas. Each year, our family would walk to the church in our village in the dark – beside the frozen reservoir, then up the hill. When we got there they would be lighting candles at the end of every pew. Then the lights went off, so there was nothing but their flickering and the pastel twinkling of the Christmas tree. One year my sister had a stomach bug, so I just went with my dad. I remember holding his hand when it started to snow. His favourite carol was always 'In the Bleak Midwinter', based on the poem 'A Christmas Carol' by Christina Rossetti:

> In the bleak midwinter, frosty wind made moan,
> Earth stood hard as iron, water like a stone;
> Snow had fallen, snow on snow, snow on snow,
> In the bleak midwinter long ago.

White Christmases were something we all dreamed of, even though snow was common then. Edgworth was high up, and we'd often get cut off by it, or the school would be shut, so we'd go sledging. Now, in London, my son reached four without even seeing snow stick to concrete – for years it pained me how common it was in his stories; how much he yearned for it.

Snow, of course, is beautiful on the page. All that clean white paper. One of the most beautiful picture books ever made is Ezra Jack Keats' *The Snowy Day* (1962), in which Peter, the protagonist, simply explores the snow in Brooklyn. The French novelist Henry de Montherlant famously claimed that happiness can't be captured in books as it 'writes in white ink on a white page', but Keats manages to catch the fleeting, swirling nature of it. The snow is torn paper, meringue. It is cities in the clouds; whipped dusklight; pearlescent, rainbow-lit like bubble bath; lilac stippled. Peter uses it as a canvas for crunchy blue tracks and snow angels. Keats used collage cut-outs made from different types of paper, handmade snowflake stamps; India ink spattered with a tooth-brush. He wrote that he was playing like a child in 'a world with no rules'.

Ezra Jack Keats changed his name in 1947 to avoid anti-Semitism. He was actually born Jacob Ezra Katz in 1916 in Brooklyn, the third child of Polish-Jewish immigrants. Although the family was very poor, Ezra was artistic from an early age, making pictures out of whatever scraps he could collect. His father, a waiter, tried to discourage his son, claiming that artists lived terrible lives, but also sometimes brought home tubes of paint, claiming: 'A starving artist swapped this for a bowl of soup.' During the Great Depression, Keats painted murals as part of the New Deal program, and backgrounds for the *Captain Marvel* comic strip. Drafted during the Second World War, he helped design camouflage patterns. Afterwards, he spent a year as a painter in Paris, before returning to New York to do commercial work, including illustrations for *Playboy* and store windows on Fifth Avenue.

The Snowy Day was only his second picture book, but it won the Caldecott Medal and became an instant classic. It is now considered a milestone for featuring one of the first African-American protagonists in a picture book. Peter was based on a series of photographs of a three- or four-year-old African-American boy about to have a blood test that Keats clipped from a May 1940 issue of *Life* magazine, then later pinned on his wall. Keats spoke of being captivated by the boy's expressive face and attitudes. Peter's dark skin and red snowsuit are indeed stunningly beautiful against the whitened city.

The book was controversial amongst civil rights activists, who had mixed reactions. The poet Langston Hughes wrote Ezra a letter praising the book and teachers wrote saying, 'The kids in my class, for the first time, are using brown crayons to draw themselves.' But many people assumed Keats was black and, he noted, 'were disappointed that I wasn't'. Nancy Larrick wrote a famous article in 1965, 'The All-White World of Children's Books', arguing that: 'Although his light skin makes him one of the world's minorities, the white child learns from his books that he is the kingfish' and railing against these 'gentle doses of racism'. In it she attacked Keats, saying the boy's mother 'is a huge figure in a gaudy yellow plaid dress, albeit without a red bandanna'. The implication was that *The Snowy Day* referenced the 'mammy' or 'Aunt Jemima' stereotype. Keats replied angrily that: 'I wish Miss Larrick would not project upon me the stereotypes in her own mind.' That she also faulted him for not using the word 'negro' seems to have particularly stung, given the anti-Semitism Keats had himself experienced. He demanded to know whether, in an illustrated book for three- to six-year-olds, where skin colour is visually apparent, it was 'necessary to append race tags? Might I suggest armbands?'

I'm glad if artists don't always default to white children; convinced by Keats when he says of Peter: 'My book would have him there simply because he should have been there all along.' But it's worth noting that *The Snowy Day* raises an ongoing problem in picture books. Representation on the page is seen as enough for the black child, or at least to tick the publisher's diversity box, yet there is (still) a staggering absence of black, Asian and minority ethnic writers and illustrators. Who gets to tell the stories is important: they get to shape our children's way of seeing the world. Almost every time I googled a supposedly 'diverse' picture book considered a classic during my research – *Handa's Surprise, Corduroy, Amazing Grace, Ten Little Fingers and Ten Little Toes* – I was uneasy when the trail led me back again and again to blinding whiteness.

In the most moving part of *The Snowy Day*, Peter makes a firm snowball and puts it in his pocket 'for tomorrow', then goes into his warm house to take off his wet socks and have a bath. Before bed he realizes: 'His pocket was empty. The snowball wasn't there. He felt very sad.' Nothing is left but a damp stain on the red suit. It seems like a first taste of transience – of mortality – but then Keats relents and ends his story hopefully. The next day the snow is replenished and Peter goes out to play in it with a friend.

Raymond Briggs must have surely had this book in mind when he wrote *The Snowman*'s famous, bleaker ending, which has left millions of children bawling with grief over their holidays. Briggs is a self-confessed hater of the season, apparently as grumpy as his depiction of Father Christmas ('BLOOMING CHIMNEYS!'), saying of Christmas Day: 'I'd like to go down into an Anderson shelter and wait for it to blow over.' He is also not that keen on children. As such he is unrepentant about the toddler tears: 'The snowman melts, my parents died, animals die, flowers die. Everything does. There's nothing particularly gloomy about it. It's a fact of life.'

By the time Briggs wrote the book he had already experienced a lot of death. Briggs was born on 18 January (also A. A. Milne's birthday) in 1934, in Wimbledon Park. His parents, the basis for his book *Ethel and Ernest*, were a milkman and a former lady's maid. Raymond himself was an evacuee at the age of five, and later did National Service. It was only after this he joined the Slade School of Art and began to illustrate. In 1963 he married a painter, Jean Taprell Clark. She had schizophrenia, 'and we got married mainly because I thought it would help her mental state – give her a feeling of stability'. His parents both died in 1971 and his wife died in 1973, of what he calls 'schizophrenia combined with leukaemia'.

Briggs has said though that: 'Schizophrenics are inspiring people. Her feelings about nature and experiences of life were very intense.' A type of psychosis, schizophrenia also means a person may not always be able to distinguish their own thoughts and ideas from reality. There is something uncanny about schizoaffective disorders: *unheimlich*. When are you speaking to the real person? When are they hacked or puppeted by 'automatic, mechanical processes'? And the sufferer themself often moves in an unhomely world. What is real? What is animate and what is inanimate? What to believe?

There is something about the cold figure of the Snowman coming to life that makes me think of the ending in Shakespeare's *The Winter's Tale*. The statue of Hermione, thought dead, beginning to breathe. The unbearable hope of it:

O, she's warm!
If this be magic, let it be an art
Lawful as eating.

The Snowman begins as an opening up of possibilities. It is about being young: it is morning; it is snowing; the world is a new canvas, waiting for us to make our marks and create something. What the boy wants to create is a companion. After building the snowman, he is excited. He wants to look at it, to be with it. He keeps getting out of bed to check on it, like a new dad checking the cot. Once the snowman comes to life he behaves like a big toddler that the boy must teach about cats and light switches and fire. He unrolls too much kitchen roll; licks ice cubes. And then the snowman seems to age, putting on the father's tie and glasses; learning to work the car. They party with games and balloons, dine together. Eventually they take flight and travel across the South Downs to Brighton, with its pavilion and pier, and watch the sunrise. It is a shared lifetime concentrated in one night.

The wordlessness is the silence of snow. It also makes it feel like a montage used in a film to show the passing of time. They hug and say goodbye.

There is a page near the end, after the boy goes to his bed, that is almost shocking in the way it holds its gaze – twelve images of a child unconscious: snuggling, writhing, changing pose. It forces us to question the reality of what we have witnessed. Has the narrative actually rewound? It appears to show us the whole story again, from a different angle – from outside rather than within the dream.

The Snowman ends with the unbearable truth of daylight. The boy is drawn with his back to us, so we cannot

see his reaction to the loss of his friend – we fill him with our own feelings; our own sorrow.

Sometimes our desire and our reality don't match. Sometimes beloved bodies fail and fall. It is an important lesson for children to learn – I know, I know – but the hardest.

Hans Christian Andersen was a cobbler's son. In his autobiography, *The Fairy Tale of My Life* (1855), he wrote of his father dying, aged just thirty-two, when Hans was eleven. In the beautiful translation by W. Glyn Jones we hear how:

> His corpse was left lying on the bed, and I slept on the floor with my mother; and a cricket chirped throughout the night. 'He is dead already,' my mother called to

it. 'You need not call to him; the Ice Maiden has taken him,' and I understood what she meant. I remembered the previous winter when our windows were frozen over; my father had shown us a figure on one of the panes like that of a maiden stretching out her arms. 'She must have come to fetch me,' he said in fun.

One of the things Andersen had left to remember his father by was a little puppet theatre he had given him, from which the sense of himself as a storyteller grew. At the age of seventy he would write, still, of that lost childhood home:

> One little room, a scullery,
> Kindliness and quiet things;
> Never a Christmas Eve like that
> In all the palaces of kings.

My own father died fifteen years ago. By then he had left the school and was running the village off-licence: his name, Albert Pollard, over the door. He was in heaven, at the centre of the village that he loved, amongst the fridges of beer, the jars of Liquorice Torpedoes, the videos he could watch over and over with no late fees; being nosey, dispensing advice and fortunes to the villagers. Totting up his profits every evening with unflagging enthusiasm: *our best Wednesday in June before 7 p.m. ever!*

That autumn, when he was given the cancer diagnosis, he said that it was because we had been too lucky.

It was over very quickly. He died at Christmas. Just a couple of days afterwards, on Christmas Eve, the village carol singers came round. They knew we were grieving and didn't want to disturb us, but sang 'In the Bleak Midwinter' in our yard, in memory of my father.

> What can I give Him, poor as I am?
> If I were a shepherd, I would bring a lamb,
> If I were a wise man, I would do my part,
> Yet what I can I give Him: give my heart.

We sat in the dark by the window, listening, tears sluicing down our faces.

My heart it melted away as snow.

Afterwards, on New Year's Eve, we buried him. It snowed that night. When I heard snow was forecast, I felt a stupid little thrill, because it *had* to be him, you see? Because it had to be a sign. Because I still believed.

But we are the snow.

Wait, though. I can't end it here.

Of course Christmas makes some grown-ups a little maudlin. When you've had too much port and a child puts her paper crown on upside down, it's hard not to mourn the moment even as you're in it. How many Christmas Days will we all have together? Since I've become a mother I can't pass an hour without seeing death everywhere: exhaust fumes, sugar, Wi-Fi radiation. I can't open a first-floor window without imagining my child plunging out of it. How am I supposed to leave a stocking full of choking hazards at the end of my daughter's cot and not wake up fretting about life's transience?

The ending of *The Snowman* aside, though, I shouldn't

project this bitter-sweet grief on to everyone. My father, an incorrigible optimist, made for the merriest Christmases: inviting over random guests who were on their own, playing Chris Rea's 'Driving Home for Christmas' at full blast, topping up everyone's glasses. When I was a child I was only conscious of Christmas as pleasure: nice food, treats, new books, family. TV as well. Normally it was just an occasional treat – *The Sooty Show, Button Moon, Rainbow, Play School* – but at Christmas the television was on for hours: *Coronation Street* specials with drawn-out death scenes, Boxing Day sport, movies. How I loved, as soon as I was old enough, to ring in biro all the shows I wanted to watch in the double-issue *Radio Times*! What happiness, to curl up next to my dad on the sofa, head against his jumper, a box of Quality Street open on the coffee table and watch reruns of *Flash Gordon* or *Live and Let Die*.

Having children has given my Christmases back some of that joy. And also joy in TV. Recently, the Christmas shows we love most as a family are based on books: *The Snowman and the Snowdog*; *We're Going on a Bear Hunt*; the 'Mog's Christmas Calamity' advert (the Sainsbury's ad, which I had to replay a zillion times on YouTube while Gruff wept at the hilarity); *Roald Dahl's Revolting Rhymes*. Then there are the Julia Donaldson and Axel Scheffler adaptations by the BBC and Magic Light, whose premieres every year on Christmas Day have become another ritual, watched on the sofa after Christmas dinner as I try to drink red wine with a child under each arm and no spillage.

The Julia Donaldson and Axel Scheffler collaborations are interesting in the story of picture books. They do not have a single, focal character in their work – like Paddington or Maisy Mouse – with most books being freestanding (give or take the odd sequel). Yet somehow Donaldson and Scheffler, a German illustrator, have become one of the strongest brands in publishing.

They first worked together on *A Squash and a Squeeze* in 1993, based on a song Donaldson wrote during her many years writing for BBC Children's TV (she even wrote songs for *Play School*), and drawing on an Eastern European Jewish folk tale. Then, in 1995, Donaldson seems to have come across a version of a traditional Chinese story, which first appears in the ancient book *Intrigues of the Warring States*, about warfare during the fifth to third centuries BC, as a political allegory about a much-feared general who is actually just claiming credit for the might of the king's army.

In the tale, a tiger is persuaded not to eat a fox after the fox insists he is more powerful. The tiger is incredulous, but the fox says that if he wants proof he only has to walk behind him. When all the animals they meet seem terrified, the tiger misinterprets this as due to the fox's reputation (rather than his own appearance) and runs away. It is a classic trickster narrative. In Chinese idiom 'a fox exploits a tiger's might' is a common phrase (狐假虎威) that has evolved from this text, and actually refers to people who turn into bullies when they have powerful connections. Donaldson metamorphosed the fox, with all its ambiguous symbolism, into a smaller, more innocent mouse and made him the hero.

'Tiger' is impossible to rhyme with (you've basically got a 'Geiger', which is a lunar impact crater on the far side of the moon, or a 'Liger', which is half lion, half tiger so feels like a cheat). Already a perfectionist in terms of rhythm and rhyming pairs, Donaldson decided she had to invent a monstrous beast too. With his 'terrible teeth' and 'terrible claws' the Gruffalo is clearly a descendant of Sendak's Wild Things. Various names were brainstormed (*Grobstrip, Shroop, Tigelephant, Wiger, Snorgle, Margelchimp* . . .) before Gruffalo was decided upon, sounding like Buffalo but fiercer ('Grrrr' being a fierce noise), and also allowing her to rhyme with 'know'. The whole tale is in a way one about the fluidity of knowledge. The mouse's lies about a Gruffalo turn out to be prophecy; his lies about being the wood's most terrifying creature also somehow become true: all the others are left shaken by their encounters with him, and the Gruffalo flees. He fakes it until he makes it, with what we 'know' exposed as assertion or illusion. The listening child, for much of the book, is also always in the position of knowing something a character on the page does not. It is a beginner's guide to dramatic irony.

The Gruffalo was sent to Reed Books in 1995, but there was no interest until Donaldson sent the text to Axel Scheffler, whom she had met only briefly since the publication of *A Squash and a Squeeze*. Within days, Alison Green at Macmillan Children's Books made an offer for

The Gruffalo. It was illustrated by Scheffler, working with a dip pen for the black outlines, then covering the drawing with ink and using coloured pencils on top, to create a meticulously detailed Germanic fairy-tale forest. His first images had the mouse wearing a Bavarian hat and Lederhosen, but Donaldson soon received a phone call from Alison asking: 'Do you envisage these animals wearing clothes?' The Gruffalo himself was based on medieval drawings and deemed too scary – Scheffler's editor told him to make the Gruffalo rounder and more 'cuddly'. The resulting creature is the perfect children's monster, a bit icky (black tongued), a bit scary (claws), but also a bit of a teddy bear. The book was finally published in 1999.

The United Kingdom's Net Book Agreement, which came into effect on 1 January 1900, involved retailers having to sell books at agreed prices. It essentially offered publishers protection from discounting, enabling them to subsidize less widely read authors with best-sellers. In many ways, I think it could be argued that protection allowed for the incredible golden age of picture books in the twentieth century, with publishers able to take creative risks with often technically complicated, full-colour books because the hungry caterpillars and clothed rabbits were subsidizing the rest. It is interesting, I think, that in March 1997, in the period in which *The Gruffalo* was lying on publishers' desks, the Restrictive Practices Court ruled that the Net Book Agreement was against the public interest and therefore illegal. Amazon, who had started trading as an online bookstore in 1995, were by then claiming to be 'the largest bookstore in the world' and began to demand rising discounts from publishers. The golden age seemed to be coming to an end.

Just two years later, *The Gruffalo*'s publication seems to herald a new kind of business model, in which Penguin Random House Children's Division can say that 'we're not just a publisher, we're a brand owner' and a creator of 'tomorrow's brands today'. In which new acquisitions depend on a 360°, transmedia approach that asks whether a character or narrative can also work as (more monetizable) films, theatre shows, toys, games or apps. Macmillan were at the forefront of this and by 2013 had even set up the fully integrated Gruffalo website: 'an online home for all aspects of the Gruffalo brand, including books, merchandise, animations and theatre' to 'further engage the Gruffalo's online community'. Admittedly, my son's name might be a factor, but Gruff has been given *The Gruffalo* as a board book, *The Gruffalo Sound Book*, *The Gruffalo Sticker Book*, *My First Gruffalo: Touch-and-Feel*, a Gruffalo jigsaw, a Gruffalo pillow and duvet set, a Gruffalo moneybox, Gruffalo snap cards. Last Christmas, we went to see *The Gruffalo* at the theatre. In 2009, 9.8 million other people sat down on Christmas Day to watch *The Gruffalo*, many likely clutching a new soft toy Owl, Snake, Mouse, Fox or (rounder, cuddlier) Gruffalo.

In many ways this is the only sensible direction for publishers. As print struggles, more are reinventing themselves as 'transmedia' organizations that also run creative writing courses, put on events, sell postcards and diaries and mugs. It is only fitting that the publishers of children's picture books, as in every great leap in publishing since they began, are at the forefront, continuing the tradition of franchising begun by creators such as Potter, Blyton and Bruna. Still, it can be a little disheartening for booklovers like myself to see shelves in bookshops given up to stuffed Elmers and Moomins. While books open up worlds, these toys seem to exist with the Octonauts amongst the realms of the too specific. A child could project so many things upon a generic toy rabbit, but a Peter Rabbit is always naughty and hopping away from Mr McGregor. He is unlikely to become, as the velveteen rabbit did, 'real'.

Scheffler and Donaldson's genius is to produce books together of such craft and quality that parents don't resent having to experience it over and over (and over) across numerous media. The repetitions of a story, now loosened from reliance on an adult's patience, can be infinite, and every one of their books is – in itself – full of structural repetitions and echoes. But perhaps our grown-up obsession with newness is mistaken anyway. If my father always retained a childlike quality, it was because if he liked something he never got bored with it. Those who enjoy rereading children's books as an adult are defended marvellously by C. S. Lewis in his essay 'On Three Ways of Writing for Children' (1952): 'I now like hock, which I am sure I should not have liked as a child. But I still like lemon-squash. I call this growth or development because I have been enriched: where I formerly had only one pleasure, now I have two.' Elsewhere, G. K. Chesterton observes:

Because children have abounding vitality, because they are in spirit fierce and free, therefore they want things repeated and unchanged. They always say, 'Do it again'; and the grown-up person does it again until he is nearly dead. For grown-up people are not strong enough to exult in monotony. But perhaps God is strong enough to exult in monotony. It is possible that God says every morning, 'Do it again' to the sun; and every evening, 'Do it again' to the moon. It may not be automatic necessity that makes all daisies alike; it may be that God makes every daisy separately, but has never got tired of making them.

Since *The Gruffalo* Donaldson and Scheffler have collaborated on *Monkey Puzzle* (2000), *Room on the Broom* (2001), *The Smartest Giant in Town* (2002), *The Snail and the Whale* (2003), *The Gruffalo's Child* (2004), *Charlie Cook's Favourite Book* (2005), *Tiddler* (2007), *Stick Man* (2008), *Tabby McTat* (2009), *Zog* (2010), *The Highway Rat* (2011), *Superworm* (2012), *The Scarecrows' Wedding* (2014), *Zog and the Flying Doctors* (2016) and *The Ugly Five* (2017). All have their charms. So many parents hymn Donaldson's skill with metre – how enjoyably and easily her poems gallop along; how after a few bedtimes you realize you have memorized them. As a poet, *The Highway Rat* is a high point for reading aloud, based on Alfred Noyes' 1906 popular poem 'The Highwayman', with its hypnotic hexameters and repetitions. I also still enjoy *Room on the Broom*, though it has been responsible for me squatting awkwardly over our broom on the kitchen tiles for long mornings, inviting my woofing/tweeting children to clamber on, then tapping it three times. On the other hand, *The Snail and the Whale* perhaps showcases Scheffler's artwork most impressively, as the pair travel the world. His pages are always rich beyond necessity with a naturalist's careful details: barnacles, acorns, stalactites, a cormorant, a heron, a flying fish, a flash of deer behind a tree, toadstools, cornflowers, toucans, a bat in the cave's corner.

Ask my daughter Cate which is her favourite, though, and the answer is unequivocal: *Stick Man*.

There is, of course, another story behind this story.

Julia Donaldson and her husband Malcolm had an eldest son, Hamish, who lived 'in his imagination'. At first Julia found this enchanting, entering into his fantasy world. He would call one of their closets an 'elevator', emerging as a different character each time he clambered into it. His reflection in the mirror became an imaginary friend called Sammy. Julia has said: 'I sometimes wonder if I entered into it too much with Hamish . . . But I think Hamish was wired differently from the start.' Soon, she noticed with growing discomfort that: 'Hamish seemed to think it was all real. And when he realized it wasn't, he lost interest. He didn't want to pretend. And he didn't want to play with Lego if all it was was Lego.'

At five he was expelled from school. Over the years they tried everything 'from psychologists to star charts' but his behaviour only became more difficult to handle, the secondary school frequently suspending him for six weeks at a time when the family could barely cope with a few hours. By sixteen he had begun to hallucinate. He talked in rhyme. He smashed the window in his room believing it was animated by malign motives.

It was reportedly one of the most severe cases of psychosis the psychiatrists had ever seen. Hamish was suffering from schizoaffective disorder. For the rest of his life he lurched from crisis to crisis, frequently hospitalized, even briefly imprisoned, with his family never knowing what he'd do next; what the phone ringing might mean. In 2003, aged twenty-five, he stepped out in front of a train. On *Desert Island Discs* Donaldson said it was 'an almost unselfish thing'.

Donaldson has also spoken of how soon afterwards, just before Christmas, Axel sent her a picture of the Gruffalo holding a candle, with the message 'A little light in the darkness'. Working on books with him was one of the ways she endured her grief. The loss is clearly present in some of the titles that come after this. *Tiddler* (2007) is the story of a young fish losing his way. Until I read Donaldson's interviews about Hamish I always wondered why Tiddler's lies about why he's late for school (treasure chests, mermaids, etc.) are not punished but celebrated, and in fact help him to find his way back when he gets caught in a net and cast out in the middle of the ocean. But they are not lies at all. They are delusions. In this fantasy, the child's difference and imagination lead him into dark, alien waters, but also, somehow, with the help of the community, bring him home (and back, even, to Julia Donaldson herself, the 'writer-friend' who appears submerged under the waters in the last page).

The loss also permeates *Stick Man*, which I think time will prove Donaldson and Scheffler's masterpiece. Stick Man is an animate stick, a husband and father to two children, his family somehow uniquely conscious when all other sticks are not. He goes out for a walk and is picked up by a dog. A series of incidents follows during which he finds himself carried further and further away from home. It becomes a kind of nursery version of *The Odyssey*, as Stick Man tries, in the face of innumerable obstacles, to get back to his family. Donaldson has said it came out of the keenness of her grieving at Christmas, and that sense that 'there's someone missing from the dinner table'. It was partly inspired by Axel Scheffler's drawing of *The Gruffalo's Child* clutching a little stick doll, but also by memories of Hamish playing with sticks during a period they lived in France – not having packed many toys, he made cardboard or twigs transform into 'ice creams or violins'.

This, then, is one of his toys brought back to life. In turn, thousands of sticks every day now are reanimated by his imagination, as little girls and boys charge through the woods with their parents, picking up ones with 'arms'. Nunhead Cemetery swarms with disorientated sticks that my daughter must help. 'Family tree, where ARE YOOOOOU?' she demands.

But the way Stick Man is mistreated by the people whom he encounters becomes increasingly upsetting as the story progresses. They use him as a sandcastle's mast, a knight's sword, a Pooh-stick – but they don't hear his voice; don't acknowledge his reality. 'I'M STICK MAN,' he protests, with increasing pathos, insisting on his humanity. Can nobody see what he sees? Is a return to the family tree just a hopeless dream? Donaldson has joked about how some people consider him an 'existential hero like something out of Sartre', but *Stick Man* might also make us think of someone with mental health issues, ignored and passed around by the system. Whose is the voice, warning him to beware of the snow? Is it the adult reading the book, the child listening (and maybe joining in to say the rhyme 'snow')? Is it the writer's own voice? Whoever warns, they are horribly impotent; never able to change his fate.

Yet the story ends with a Christmas miracle. This is not *The Snowman*. Donaldson has said: 'I am not keen on those old fairy tales where children end up being boiled in a pot by a troll. Children need hope and a belief you can overcome difficulties.' Stick Man falls unconscious in the snow by the side of the road, skinny and yellow-eyed. A carol singer puts him in the grate. Then in the night, before the fire is lit, he hears something in the chimney: a 'stuck' man. In selflessly struggling to free him, Stick Man also saves himself.

It is Santa Claus who is stuck, and once freed he asks Stick Man to help him deliver presents to boys and girls (the same ones, perhaps, who used him so cruelly earlier on). And then we cut to the family tree, so beautifully imagined by Scheffler – the pencilled 'stick' figures on the walls, the acorn pull-along toy, the silver birch bed with its blanket of leaves. The window they stared hope-fully from all year that feels like a tear; a painful wound. The small, sad faces of the children as their mother tucks them in. It doesn't feel like Christmas 'without their Stick Dad'.

Only then there is a sudden sound above them.

> Someone is tumbling into their house.
> Is it a bird, or a bat, or a mouse?
> Or could it . . . yes, could it just possibly be . . .

It is always happy endings that make me cry the most, my voice turning shrill and broken as I read them – espe-cially happy endings where the characters are back where they began. How to explain this to a child?

Darling, it's because all they want is what they had; to repeat it over.

Coda

The most important picture book of the last few years is, for me, *Malala's Magic Pencil* (2017) by Malala Yousafzai, illustrated by Kerascoët. In it Malala, an activist who was shot by a masked Taliban gunman on a bus, aged fifteen, tells of how when she was younger she wanted a magic pencil – one that could erase the stink of refuse or conjure up a football for her to play with. The book contains truths we have always instinctively kept from Western children: boys so poor they fish for scraps of metal on flyblown rubbish dumps; men who stalk the streets carrying weapons. Malala has said in an interview that it was important for her that the art: 'felt accurate, down to the cracks in the wall of our home (I had to ask them to add more cracks)'. Yet it is also hopeful, telling us that words are magical and can change the world. The very act of her recounting her own story, as both a young Pakistani woman and a Nobel Prize winner, through the medium of a picture book, is significant. 'My voice became so powerful that dangerous men tried to silence me,' she tells us. 'But they failed.'

We diminish the preschool years. For parents, they're framed as a period of teething, sleeplessness and career stagnation that will 'get easier' once the children start school; portrayed as both tedious and fleeting – some-how, days are both endless yet gone 'before you know it'. Toddlers, people say, don't recall anything before they're four anyway. Small children's culture is seen as mean-ingless, trivial, saccharine, something to shut them up or keep them busy. But this is because our society does not place enough value on children, women, home, care, patience or poetry. It is also because our society refuses to accept responsibility for the adults it makes. We are lucky that some of the geniuses in this history knew that picture books are not a minor form, but one of the most important of all. A picture book can, like a fierce bad rabbit, look innocent but conceal darker forces. It can also teach us empathy, heroism and love.

By the time I started school, I was myself. I look at photos of that girl, her wilful fringe and dreamy, serious expression, and know that I have changed very little, and that who I am was shaped by my mother and father; by the books that they read to me.

Before I finish, I'm aware there is an author I haven't mentioned yet, one who was younger even than Malala Yousafzai. Jayne Fisher, creator of the *Garden Gang* books, published by Ladybird from 1979–83, with the first written when she was nine years old. How I loved those felt-tipped drawings of Penelope Strawberry, with her fine golden hairs; her garden party with Blancmange and hundreds of sausage rolls. Roger Radish saving the two little chives from drowning. That cross-eyed pea; the elegance of Grace Grape; little blackberries waiting for their socks to dry.

I have tried to track her down to no avail. There are few clues on the Internet to what became of her. All I know of Jayne Fisher is the profile at the beginning of each book – her centre-parted hair, polo neck and cord dungarees. Her hobbies (classical guitar, the recorder, sewing, baking and chess). She kept two gerbils and bred stick insects. She based the stories 'on her own little garden at home'.

Oh dear, sweet, ambitious Jayne! How ardently I wanted to be like her, to compete with her: a prodigy, a *real* writer. Of all the picture books that inspired me, it is perhaps to these I owe the biggest debt, because I looked at her photo and things became possible. After 'writing' (mainly in my head) my first play at four, *The Little Goose Girl*, in infants I also wrote two long tales down in notepads: *The Scruffs*, about messy kids who get into scrapes, and the melodramatic epic *Gipsy Horse*. Then came the 'Lisa Spector' series, where the daughter of an oil magnate has adventures in exotic locations – Transylvania, the Bermuda Triangle, Egypt, New York – and which my Granny Cranshaw would type up on her typewriter for my birthday. In *Hard Cheddar* mice plotted the murder of all the world's cats. *Sand Up My Nostrils* tackled evil genies. Somewhere along the line, I got the idea that for it to be a novel you had to reach 100 pages, and near the end my handwriting would get VERY BIG. I could magic up adventures; entire worlds. I had found my vocation.

My dad always predicted I would be a writer. I have said I don't know what my father really believed in, but that isn't quite true. I know he believed in me.

Listen, they say that time isn't really linear: it's just a human invention; another story we teach our children to help them make sense of this world. Norman Warne is giving Beatrix Potter doll's house furniture, Christopher Robin sleeps hugging his bear, a one-year-old sees a rabbit hop through the dunes, a ladybird takes wing, Janet Ahlberg paints a gingerbread bungalow, a coachman's wife recounts witchcraft, a mother talks tiger.

The milk is poured; we snuggle on the bed. I am forty and I am four. As I read the story to my children, my father reads the story to me again, and yes, we are lucky.

Bibliography

Picture books referred to by chapter

Introduction

Hilda Boswell, *Hilda Boswell's Treasury of Poetry* (William Collins, 1968)

1. The Butterfly's Ball

Jez Alborough, *Where's My Teddy?* (Walker Books, 1992)

Hans Christian Andersen, trans. Tina Nunnally, *Fairy Tales* (Penguin, 2004)

Hilaire Belloc, *Cautionary Tales for Children* (1907) (Duckworth, 1957)

Randolph Caldecott, *The Babes in the Wood* (Routledge, 1879)

Lewis Carroll and John Tenniel, *Alice's Adventures in Wonderland* (Macmillan, 1865)

Lewis Carroll and John Tenniel, *Through the Looking-Glass* (Macmillan, 1871)

Julia Donaldson and Axel Scheffler, *The Smartest Giant in Town* (Macmillan, 2002)

Edward Gorey, *Gashlycrumb Tinies* (Simon and Schuster, 1963)

Kate Greenaway, *The Language of Flowers* (Routledge, 1884)

Kate Greenaway and Robert Browning, *The Pied Piper of Hamelin* (Routledge, 1888)

Heinrich Hoffmann, *Der Struwwelpeter* (Frederick Warne, 1884)

Edward Lear, *A Book of Nonsense* (Thomas McLean, 1846)

Edward Lear, *Nonsense Songs* (Robert John Bush, 1870)

Edward Lear, *More Nonsense* (Robert John Bush, 1872)

Edward Lear, *Laughable Lyrics* (Robert John Bush, 1877)

John Newbery, *A Little Pretty Pocket-Book* (John Newbery, 1744)

William Roscoe, *The Butterfly's Ball, and the Grasshopper's Feast* (J. Harris, 1808)

2. 'Ourselves in fur'

Helen Bannerman, *The Story of Little Black Sambo* (Grant Richards, 1899)

Elvira Bauer and Philipp Rupprecht, *Trust No Fox on his Green Heath and No Jew on his Oath* (Stürmer-Verlag, 1936)

Margaret Wise Brown and Clement Hurd, *The Runaway Bunny* (1942) (HarperCollins, 2013)

Margaret Wise Brown and Clement Hurd, *Goodnight Moon* (1947) (Two Hoots, 2017)

Margaret Wise Brown and Alice and Martin Provensen, *The Color Kittens* (1949) (Random House, 2003)

Margaret Wise Brown and Garth Williams, *Little Fur Family* (Harper & Brothers, 1946)

Dick Bruna trans. Patricia Crampton, *Miffy at School* (1988) (World International, 1997)

Dick Bruna trans. Tony Mitton, *Miffy* (Simon & Schuster, 2014)

Jean de Brunhoff, *The Story of Babar* (1931) (Egmont, 2008)

Jean de Brunhoff, *Babar's Travels* (1932) (Egmont, 2008)

Jean de Brunhoff, *Babar the King* (1933) (Egmont, 2008)

Randolph Caldecott, *Hey-Diddle-Diddle and Baby Bunting* (George Routledge & Sons, 1882)

Munro Leaf and Robert Lawson, *The Story of Ferdinand* (Viking, 1936)

Sam McBratney and Anita Jeram's *Guess How Much I Love You* (Walker Books, 1994)

Beatrix Potter, *The Complete Tales* (Frederick Warne, 2012)

Alison Uttley and Margaret Tempest, *The Little Grey Rabbit Treasury* (Heinemann, 1993)

Charlotte Zolotow and Maurice Sendak, *Mr Rabbit and the Lovely Present* (1962) (Red Fox, 2002)

3. I Know How a Jam Jar Feels

Ronda and David Armitage, *The Lighthouse Keeper's Lunch* (Scholastic, 1977)

Eileen Browne, *Handa's Surprise* (Walker, 1994)

Janet Burroway and John Vernon Lord, *The Giant Jam Sandwich* (Houghton Mifflin, 1972)

Eric Carle, *The Very Hungry Caterpillar* (1969) (Puffin, 2002)

Eric Carle and Bill Martin Jr, *Brown Bear, Brown Bear, What Do You See?* (1967) (Puffin, Anniversary Edition, 2007)

Trish Cooke and Paul Howard, *Full, Full, Full of Love* (Walker, 2003)

Mem Fox and Julie Vivas, *Possum Magic* (Scholastic, 1983)

Russell and Lillian Hoban, *Bread and Jam for Frances* (1964) (HarperCollins, 2008)

Judith Kerr, *The Tiger Who Came to Tea* (1968) (HarperCollins, Anniversary Edition, 2018)

Peter Newell, *The Hole Book* (Harper & Brothers, 1908)

Maurice Sendak, *In the Night Kitchen* (1970) (Red Fox, 2001)

Maurice Sendak, *Outside Over There* (1981) (Red Fox, 2002)

Dr Seuss, *Horton Hears a Who!* (1954) (HarperCollins, 2016)

Dr Seuss, *Green Eggs and Ham* (1960) (HarperCollins, 2016)

Dr Seuss, *The Cat in the Hat* (1957) (HarperCollins, 2016)

Dr Seuss, *Oh, The Places You'll Go* (1990) (HarperCollins, 2016)

Martin Waddell and Helen Oxenbury, *Farmer Duck* (Walker, 1995)

4. The Wild Rumpus

Janet and Allan Ahlberg, *Burglar Bill* (Heinemann, 1977)

Janet and Allan Ahlberg, *Each Peach Pear Plum* (Kestrel, 1978)

Janet and Allan Ahlberg, *Funnybones* (Heinemann, 1980)

Janet and Allan Ahlberg, *Peepo!* (Viking, 1981)

Janet and Allan Ahlberg, *The Jolly Postman* (Heinemann, 1986)

Janet and Allan Ahlberg, *It Was a Dark and Stormy Night* (Viking, 1993)

John Fardell, *The Day Louis Got Eaten* (Andersen Press, 2012)

Tom Fletcher, Dougie Poynter and Garry Parsons, *The Dinosaur that Pooped a Planet* (Random House Children's, 2013)

Claire Freedman and Ben Cort, *Aliens Love Underpants* (Simon & Schuster, 2007)

Claire Freedman and Ben Cort, *Pirates Love Underpants* (Simon & Schuster, 2013)

Claire Freedman and Ben Cort, *Monsters Love Underpants* (Simon & Schuster, 2015)

Taro Gomi, *Everybody Poos* (1977) (Frances Lincoln, 2012)

Russell and Lillian Hoban, *Best Friends for Frances* (1969) (Puffin, 1978)

Werner Holzwarth and Wolf Erlbruch, *The Story of the Little Mole Who Knew it Was None of His Business* (David Bennett Books, 1994)

Jon Klassen, *I Want My Hat Back* (Walker Books, 2011)

David McKee, *Not Now, Bernard* (1980) (Andersen Press, 2015)

David McKee, *Elmer* (1989) (Andersen Press, Anniversary Edition, 2019)

David McKee, *Denver* (2010) (Andersen Press, 2012)

David McKee, *Melric* (Ladybird, 2013)

Hiawyn Oram and Satoshi Kitamura, *Angry Arthur* (Andersen Press, 1982)

Richard Scarry, *Cars and Trucks and Things That Go* (1974) (HarperCollins, 2010)

Maurice Sendak, *Where the Wild Things Are* (1963) (Red Fox, 2000)

Dr Seuss, *The Lorax* (Random House, 1972) (HarperCollins, 2016)

Elfrida Vipont and Raymond Briggs, *The Elephant and the Bad Baby* (1979) (Puffin, 2016)

Jeanne Willis and Tony Ross, *Tadpole's Promise* (Andersen Press, 2003)

5. My Little Eye

Janet and Allan Ahlberg, *Peepo!* (Viking, 1981)

Jez Alborough, *Some Dogs Do* (Walker, 2004)

Jonathan Allen, *I'm Not Scared* (Boxer Books, 2008)

Jan and Stan Berenstain, *The Big Honey Hunt* (Random House, 1962)

Jan and Stan Berenstain, *The Bears' Picnic* (Random House, 1966)

Jan and Stan Berenstain, *The Birds and the Bees and the Berenstain Bears* (Random House, 2000)

Anthony Browne, *Gorilla* (1983) (Walker, 1992)

Anthony Browne, *Changes* (1990) (Walker, 2008)

Anthony Browne, *My Dad* (2000) (Doubleday, 2003)

Dick Bruna trans. Tony Mitton, *Miffy and the New Baby* (Simon & Schuster, 2014)

Rod Campbell, *Dear Zoo* (Macmillan, 1982)

Lucy Cousins, *Peck, Peck, Peck* (Walker, 2016)

Eric Hill, *Where's Spot?* (1980) (Frederick Warne, 1998)

Tim Hopgood, *WOW! Said the Owl* (Macmillan, 2016)

Shirley Hughes, *Lucy & Tom's Day* (1960) (Puffin, 1973)

Shirley Hughes, *Dogger* (1977) (Red Fox, 2009)

Shirley Hughes, *Alfie Gets in First* (1981) (Red Fox, 2009)

Jill Murphy, *Five Minutes' Peace* (Walker Books, 1986)

Jill Murphy, *Mr Large in Charge* (Walker Books, 2005)

Michael Rosen and Helen Oxenbury, *We're Going on a Bear Hunt* (1989) (Walker Books, 1997)

Martin Waddell and Patrick Benson, *Owl Babies* (Walker Books, 1992)

Martin Waddell and Barbara Firth, *Can't You Sleep, Little Bear?* (1988) (Walker Books, 2013)

6. The Glass Castle

My Book of Elves and Fairies (Collins, undated)

Cicely Mary Barker, *Flower Fairies of the Spring* (1923) (Blackie & Son, 1974)

Cicely Mary Barker, *Flower Fairies of the Wayside* (1948) (Blackie & Son, 1974)

Babette Cole, *Princess Smartypants* (Puffin, 1986)

Julia Donaldson and Axel Scheffler, *Zog* (Alison Green, 2010)

Julia Donaldson and Axel Scheffler, *Zog and the Flying Doctors* (Alison Green, 2016)

Elena Favilli and Francesca Cavallo, *Good Night Stories for Rebel Girls* (Particular Books, 2017)

Roger Hargreaves and Adam Hargreaves, *Mr Men: My Complete Collection Box Set* (Egmont, 2013)

Roger Hargreaves and Adam Hargreaves, *Little Miss: The Complete Collection* (Egmont, 2014)

Robert Munsch and Sheila McGraw, *Love You Forever* (Firefly Books, 1986).

Robert Munsch and Michael Martchenko, *The Paper Bag Princess* (Annick Press, 1980)

Helen Nicoll and Jan Pieńkowski, *Meg and Mog* (Heinemann, 1972)

Helen Nicoll and Jan Pieńkowski, *Meg's Eggs* (Heinemann, 1972)

María Isabel Sánchez Vegara, *Frida Kahlo (Little People, Big Dreams)* (Frances Lincoln, 2018)

Vera Southgate and Robert Lumley, *The Elves and the Shoe-maker* (Ladybird, 1965)

Vera Southgate and Eric Winter, *Snow White and Rose Red* (Ladybird, 1969)

Fiona Watt and Rachel Wells, *That's Not My Princess* (Usborne, 2006)

7. Snow Angels

Enid Blyton and Beek, *Noddy Goes to Toyland* (Sampson Low, 1949)

Enid Blyton and Beek, *Here Comes Noddy Again!* (Sampson Low, 1951)

Enid Blyton and Olive F. Openshaw, *The Adventures of Mary Mouse* (Brockhampton Press, 1942–64)

Raymond Briggs, *The Snowman* (Hamish Hamilton, 1978)

Julia Donaldson and Axel Scheffler, *A Squash and a Squeeze* (Macmillan, 1993)

Julia Donaldson and Axel Scheffler, *The Gruffalo* (Macmillan, 1999)

Julia Donaldson and Axel Scheffler, *Room on the Broom* (Macmillan, 2001)

Julia Donaldson and Axel Scheffler, *The Snail and the Whale* (Macmillan, 2003)

Julia Donaldson and Axel Scheffler, *The Gruffalo's Child* (Macmillan, 2004)

Julia Donaldson and Axel Scheffler, *Tiddler* (Alison Green Books, 2007)

Julia Donaldson and Axel Scheffler, *Stick Man* (Alison Green Books, 2008)

Julia Donaldson and Axel Scheffler, *The Highway Rat* (Alison Green Books, 2011)

E. T. A Hoffmann (trans. Ralph Manheim) and Maurice Sendak, *The Nutcracker* (Crown Publishers, 1984)

Ezra Jack Keats, *The Snowy Day* (1962) (Puffin, 1986)

A. A. Milne and E. H. Shepard, *Winnie-the-Pooh* (Methuen, 1926)

A. A. Milne and E. H. Shepard, *The House at Pooh Corner* (Methuen, 1928)

William Nicholson, *Clever Bill* (William Heinemann, 1926)

Bertha Upton and Florence K. Upton, *The Adventure of Two Dutch Dolls and a 'Golliwogg'* (Longmans, Green & Co., 1895)

Margery Williams and William Nicholson, *The Velveteen Rabbit* (1922) (Egmont, 2007)

Coda

Jayne Fisher, *Penelope Strawberry and Roger Radish* (Ladybird, 1979)

Malala Yousafzai and Kerascoët, *Malala's Magic Pencil* (Puffin, 2017)

Other Sources

Allan Ahlberg, 'The 2016 Philippa Pearce Lecture: John Wayne and Sibelius *or* The Train Has Rain in It' (text of lecture read at the Mary Allan Building, Homerton College, Cambridge, Thursday 1 September 2016)

Allan Ahlberg, *Janet's Last Book* (Penguin, 1997)

Allan Ahlberg, *The Bucket: Memories of an Inattentive Childhood* (Viking, 2013)

Decca Aitkenhead, 'Raymond Briggs: "There could be another world war. Terrifying, isn't it?"', in *The Guardian* (24 December 2016)

Lisa Allardice, 'Bunny Love', in *The Guardian* (15 Feb 2006)

Lisa Allardice, 'Julia Donaldson and Axel Scheffler: "The Gruffalo's not a curse . . . it can be a burden"', in *The Guardian* (22 September 2017)

David A. Anderson and Mykol Hamilton, 'Gender Role Stereotyping of Parents in Children's Picture Books: The Invisible Father', in *Sex Roles*, Volume 52, Issues 3–4, (February 2005)

Arthur N. Applebee, *The Child's Concept of Story* (University of Chicago Press, 1978)

Roland Barthes, trans. Annette Lavers, *Mythologies* (Hill & Wang, 1973)

Mary Beard, 'The Book That Made Me a Feminist', in *The Guardian* (16 December 2017)

Bruno Bettelheim, *The Uses of Enchantment: The Meaning and Importance of Fairy Tales* (Alfred A. Knopf, 1977)

Margaret Blount, *Animal Land: The Creatures of Children's Fiction* (Hutchinson & Co, 1974)

Rebecca Bramall, 'Memory, Meaning and Multi-directionality: Remembering Austerity Britain', in Noakes, L. and Pattinson, J., eds, *British Cultural Memory and the Second World War* (Bloomsbury, 2013)

Daisy Bridgewater, 'Going on a Bear Hunt', in *The Telegraph* (7 June 2014)

Charlie Brooker, 'The Mr Men Inhabit a Godless Universe. It's a Brutal Existence', in *The Guardian* (2 June 2014)

Anthony Browne with Joe Browne, *Playing the Shape Game* (Doubleday, 2011)

Dorothy Butler, *Babies Need Books* (Penguin, 1980)

Joey Canessa, 'Me and My Home: Once Upon a Time', in *The Independent* (23 March 2005)

Eric Carle, 'The Art of Fiction No. 229', in *The Paris Review for Younger Readers* (Spring 2015)

Eric Carle, *The Art of Eric Carle* (Penguin, 1996)

Roderick Cave and Sara Ayad, *A History of Children's Books in 100 Books* (British Library, 2017)

G. K. Chesterton, *The Defendant* (R. Brimley Johnson, 1901)

G. K. Chesterton, *Orthodoxy* (Bodley Head, 1908)

Jonathan Cott, *There's a Mystery There* (Doubleday, 2017)

Sarah Crown, 'A Life in Books: Anthony Browne', in *The Guardian* (3 July 2009)

Sarah Crown, 'How we Made: Julia Donaldson and Axel Scheffler on The Gruffalo', in *The Guardian* (30 Jan 2012)

Danielle Davis, 'Taro Gomi's Picture Book Life', on this picturebooklife.com (14 July 2015). Accessed 22 January 2019

Lesley Delaney, 'Walter Crane: a revolution in nursery picture books', in *Books for Keeps* (November, 2010)

Matthew Dennison, *Over the Hills and Far Away: The Life of Beatrix Potter* (Head of Zeus, 2017)

Rita Dove, 'After Reading *Mickey in the Night Kitchen* for the Third Time Before Bed', in *Grace Notes* (W. W. Norton, 1991)

Arthur Conan Doyle, *The Coming of the Fairies* (Hodder and Stoughton, 1922)

Julia Eccleshare, ed., *1001 Children's Books You Must Read Before You Grow Up* (Quintessence, 2009)

Rodney Engen, *Kate Greenaway: A Biography* (MacDonald, 1981)

Cordelia Fine, *Delusions of Gender* (Icon Books, 2011)

F. Scott Fitzgerald, *The Great Gatsby* (Charles Scribner's Sons, 1925)

Alison Flood, 'Diaries Reveal Dark Side to Little Grey Rabbit's Creator', in *The Guardian* (17 June 2009)

Alison Flood, 'Meg, Mog and Other Monsters', in *The Guardian* (22 December 2008)

Alison Flood, 'Spot the Dog Creator Eric Hill Dies Aged 86', in *The Guardian* (10 June 2014)

Sigmund Freud, 'The Uncanny' (1919) in *The Uncanny* (Penguin, 2003)

Sigmund Freud, 'Beyond the Pleasure Principle' (1920) in *Beyond the Pleasure Principle: And Other Writings* (Penguin Modern Classics, 2003)

Amy Gary, *In the Great Green Room: The Brilliant and Bold Life of Margaret Wise Brown* (Flatiron, 2017)

Adam Gopnik, 'Freeing the Elephants: What Babar brought', in *The New Yorker* (22 September 2008)

Richard M. Gottlieb, MD, 'Maurice Sendak's Trilogy', in *The Psychoanalytic Study of the Child*, Volume 63, Issue 1 (2008)

Graham Greene, 'Beatrix Potter' (1933) and 'The Lost Childhood' (1947) in *Collected Essays* (Vintage, 1999)

Bruce Handy, *Wild Things: The Joy of Reading Children's Literature as an Adult* (Simon and Schuster, 2018)

Adam Hargreaves, 'Interview with Adam Hargreaves', in *Sussex Life* (15 February 2010)

E. T. A. Hoffmann, 'The Sandman' (1816) *in Die Nachtstücke* (The Night Pieces) (1817)

Mary Hoffmann, 'The Princess Problem', in *The Guardian* (12 October 2007)

Kathleen T. Horning, 'The Enduring Footprints of Peter, Ezra Jack Keats, and The Snowy Day', in *The Horn Book* (7 July 2016)

Shirley Hughes, *What Do Artists Do All Day?* Documentary on BBC Four (18 July 2016)

Bettina Hürlimann, trans. Brian W. Alderson, *Three Centuries of Children's Books in Europe* (OUP, 1967)

Adam Jacques, 'How We Met: Julia Donaldson and Axel Scheffler', in *The Independent* (13 January 2013)

Nicolette Jones, 'The Renaissance of Beatrix Potter's Great Rival', in *The Telegraph* (16 January 2015)

Sheila Glyn Jones, *Cicely Mary Barker: A Croydon Artist* (Croydon Natural History & Scientific Society, 1989)

Denis Judd, *Alison Uttley: Spinner of Tales* (Manchester University Press, 2010)

Kate Kellaway, 'It Began with a Shaggy Dog Story', in *The Observer* (15 July 2007)

Judith Kerr, *When Hitler Stole Pink Rabbit* (William Collins, 1971)

Judith Kerr, *Judith Kerr's Creatures* (HarperCollins, 2013)

Tracy King, 'Sorry Little Miss Inventor, but You're Misterland's Token Feminist', in the *New Statesman* (23 November 2017)

Herbert Kohl, *Should we Burn Babar?* (The New Press, 1995)

Jane Laing, *Cicely Mary Barker and Her Art* (Frederick Warne, 1995)

Nancy Larrick, 'The All-White World of Children's Books', *Saturday Review* (11 September 1965)

Laurie Lee, *Cider with Rosie* (1959) (Vintage, 2014)

C. S. Lewis, 'On Three Ways of Writing for Children' (1952) in *Of Other Worlds: Essays and Stories* (First Harvest, 1975)

Federico García Lorca, 'On Lullabies' (1928), trans. A. S. Kline (2008), on https://www.poetryintranslation.com/PITBR/Spanish/Lullabies.php. Accessed 22 January 2019

Alison Lurie, *Boys and Girls Forever* (Vintage, 2011)

Alison Lurie, *Not in Front of the Grown-ups* (Cardinal, 1990)

Gregory Maguire, *Making Mischief: A Maurice Sendak Appreciation* (HarperCollins, 2009)

Noel Malcolm, *The Origins of English Nonsense* (HarperCollins, 1997)

Lucy Mangan, *Bookworm* (Square Peg, 2018)

Leonard S. Marcus, *Minders of Make-Believe* (Houghton Mifflin, 2008)

Leonard S. Marcus, *Ways of Telling: Conversations on the Art of the Picture Book* (Dutton, 2002)

Leonard S. Marcus, *Randolph Caldecott* (Frances Foster Books, 2013)

Elizabeth Mehren, 'The Bear Facts', in the *LA Times* (1 Feb 1995)

Julia Mickenberg and Lyne Vallone, *The Oxford Handbook of Children's Literature* (OUP, 2011)

Ann Montanaro, 'A Concise History of Pop-up and Movable Books', on www.libraries.rutgers.edu. Accessed 20 June 2018

Neil and Judith Morgan, *Dr Seuss and Mr Geisel* (Random House, 1995)

Rosie Murray-West, 'Hargreaves in the Money with Sale of Mr Men', in *The Telegraph* (1 May 2004)

Vivien Noakes, *Edward Lear: The Life of a Wanderer* (The History Press, 2006)

Alfred Noyes, *Forty Singing Seamen and Other Poems* (W. Blackwood and Sons, 1907)

NPR Staff, 'The Snowy Day: Breaking Color Barriers Quietly', on www.NPR.org (28 January 2012). Accessed 22 January 2019

Iona and Peter Opie, *The Lore and Language of Schoolchildren* (OUP, 1959)

Dorothy Parker, 'Far from Well' (1928), in *The Collected Dorothy Parker*, ed. Brendan Gill (Penguin, 1973)

Jan Michelle Pauli, 'Allan Ahlberg – A Life in Writing', in *The Guardian* (30 April 2011)

Nina Perry, *The Universal Language of Lullabies*, for the BBC World Service (21 January 2013)

Jan Pieńkowski, 'Helen Nicoll Obituary', in *The Guardian* (9 October 2012)

Candice Pires, 'On the prowl: inside the home of the author of The Tiger Who Came to Tea', in *The Guardian* (4 March 2017)

Max Porter, 'Angry Arthur by Hiawyn Oram & Satoshi Kitamura, Book of a Lifetime', in *The Independent* (1 October 2015)

Philip Pullman, *Daemon Voices* (David Fickling, 2017)

Lindsay Quayle, 'Bookbug Author Spotlight: Martin Waddell', in *Bookbug* (21 June 2016)

Suzanne Rahn, 'Cat-Quest: A Symbolic Animal in Margaret Wise Brown', in *Children's Literature*, Volume 22, 1994

Juliet Rix, 'Shirley Hughes: It is difficult to protect today's youngsters from being overstimulated', in *The Telegraph* (10 July 2017)

Anne Rooney, 'Not Now, Bernard – David McKee', on the *Stroppy Author: Book Vivisection* blog (18 June 2012). Accessed 22 January 2019

David Rudd, *Enid Blyton and the Mystery of Children's Literature* (Palgrave Macmillan, 2000)

Martin Salisbury with Morag Styles, *Children's Picture Books: The Art of Visual Storytelling* (Lawrence King, 2012)

Jessica Salter, 'The World of Allan Ahlberg, Author', in *The Telegraph* (6 September 2013)

Maurice Sendak, *Caldecott & Co.: Notes on Books and Pictures* (Noonday Press, 1990)

Dr Seuss, 'My Hassle with the First Grade Language', in *The Chicago Tribune* (17 November 1957)

Imogen Smallwood, *A Childhood at Green Hedges* (Methuen, 1989)

Ellen Handler Spitz, *Inside Picture Books* (Yale University Press, 2000)

Francis Spufford, *The Child that Books Built* (Faber & Faber, 2003)

James Sturcke, 'Golliwog Began as Beloved Children's Character', in *The Guardian* (5 Feb 2009)

Bryan Talbot, *Alice in Sunderland* (Jonathan Cape, 2007)

Dylan Thomas and Edward Ardizzone, *A Child's Christmas in Wales* (Dolphin, 1978)

Ann Thwaite, *Goodbye Christopher Robin* (Pan Books, 2017)

Anna Tims, 'How we made: Helen Oxenbury and Michael Rosen on We're Going on a Bear Hunt', in *The Guardian* (5 November 2012)

Jenny Uglow, 'The Lure of Illustrated Children's Books', in *The Guardian* (9 December 2009)

Jenny Uglow, *Mr Lear* (Faber & Faber, 2017)

Alison Uttley, *The Country Child* (1931) (Puffin, 2016)

Ed Vulliamy, 'My grandad's store and the end of the high street', in *The Observer* (3 July 2011)

Mark Waldron, 'The Sausage Factory' in *The Brand New Dark* (Salt, 2008)

Lucy Wallis, 'Judith Kerr and the story behind The Tiger Who Came to Tea', *BBC News* (26 November 2013)

John Walsh, 'Ripping Yarns: Enid Blyton's Secret Life', in *The Independent* (14 March 2009)

John Walsh, 'Raymond Briggs: Seasonal Torment for the Snowman Creator', in *The Independent* (21 December 2012)

Marina Warner, *Signs and Wonders: Essays on Literature and Culture* (Vintage, 2004)

Marina Warner, *Once Upon a Time* (OUP, 2016)

Marina Warner, *Managing Monsters* (Vintage, 1994)

Sally Williams, 'Beatrix Potter's Nemesis', in *The Independent* (7 December 1997)

Rachel Wilson, 'Martin Waddell – A Child for Forty Years' on culturenorthernireland.org (10 April 2008). Accessed 22 January 2019

Bee Wilson, *First Bite* (Fourth Estate, 2016)

Frances Wilson, 'The Private Diaries of Alison Uttley edited by Denis Judd', in *The Sunday Times* (19 July 2009)

Nicholas Wroe, 'A Life in Books: Shirley Hughes', in *The Guardian* (6 March 2009)

Malala Yousafzai, 'Young readers should never doubt themselves if they are fighting injustice', on www.penguin.co.uk (2 October 2017). Accessed 22 January 2019

Jack Zipes, *Sticks and Stones: The Troublesome Success of Children's Literature from Slovenly Peter to Harry Potter* (Routledge, 2001)

Jack Zipes, ed. and trans., *The Original Folk and Fairy Tales of the Brothers Grimm* (Princeton University Press, 2014)

I have also made extensive use of Wikipedia as a starting point for research, so many thanks to all the anonymous academics and enthusiasts who make it such a rich resource in relation to picture books.

Our Favourite Fifty Picture Books

For anyone who wants to start a library, here is a very personal, partial list of what I think are the fifty best picture books to read with young children (up to six). These are not the most historically or artistically important – those are listed in the bibliography – but rather the ones that I have enjoyed sharing with Gruff and Cate, that I think you will find yourself reading again and again.

Janet and Allan Ahlberg, *Burglar Bill*

Janet and Allan Ahlberg, *Funnybones*

Ronda and David Armitage, *The Lighthouse Keeper's Lunch*

Jan and Stan Berenstain, *The Bears' Picnic*

Michael Bond and R. W. Alley, *Paddington Bear*

Margaret Wise Brown and Alice and Martin Provensen, *The Color Kittens*

Margaret Wise Brown and Clement Hurd, *Goodnight Moon*

Anthony Browne, *Gorilla*

Eileen Browne, *Handa's Surprise*

John Burningham, *Avocado Baby*

Janet Burroway and John Vernon Lord, *The Giant Jam Sandwich*

Rod Campbell, *Dear Zoo*

Eric Carle, *The Very Hungry Caterpillar*

Eric Carle and Bill Martin Jr, *Brown Bear, Brown Bear, What Do You See?*

Trish Cooke and Paul Howard, *Full, Full, Full of Love*

Lucy Cousins, *Peck, Peck, Peck*

Lynley Dodd, *Hairy Maclary from Donaldson's Dairy*

Julia Donaldson and Axel Scheffler, *Stick Man*

John Fardell, *The Day Louis Got Eaten*

Taro Gomi, *Everybody Poos*

Emily Gravett, *The Odd Egg*

Kes Gray and Jim Field, *Oi Frog!*

Chris Haughton, *Oh No, George!*

Eric Hill, *Where's Spot?*

Russell Hoban and Lillian Hoban, *Bread and Jam for Frances*

Mary Hoffman and Caroline Binch, *Amazing Grace*

Shirley Hughes, *Dogger*

Pat Hutchins, *Rosie's Walk*

Dahlov Ipcar, *I Like Animals*

Oliver Jeffers, *Stuck*

Ezra Jack Keats, *The Snowy Day*

Judith Kerr, *Mog's Christmas*

Judith Kerr, *The Tiger Who Came to Tea*

Jon Klassen, *I Want My Hat Back*

David McKee, *Not Now, Bernard*

Robert Munsch and Michael Martchenko, *The Paper Bag Princess*

Jill Murphy, *Peace at Last*

Helen Nicoll and Jan Pieńkowski, *Meg's Eggs*

Hiawyn Oram and Satoshi Kitamura, *Angry Arthur*

Beatrix Potter, *The Tale of Peter Rabbit*

Michael Rosen and Helen Oxenbury, *We're Going on a Bear Hunt*

Richard Scarry, *Cars and Trucks and Things That Go*

Maurice Sendak, *In the Night Kitchen*

Maurice Sendak, *Where the Wild Things Are*

Dr Seuss, *Green Eggs and Ham*

Dr Seuss, *There's a Wocket in my Pocket!*

Nick Sharratt and Pippa Goodhart, *You Choose*

Elfrida Vipont and Raymond Briggs, *The Elephant and the Bad Baby*

Martin Waddell and Patrick Benson, *Owl Babies*

Martin Waddell and Helen Oxenbury, *Farmer Duck*

Acknowledgements

Enormous thanks are due to the many people who helped with this book. To my agent, Jenny Hewson, who encouraged me to put together the pitch, and without whom it wouldn't exist. To Assallah Tahir and Juliet Annan at Fig Tree for their warm support and scrupulous line edits. To the Royal Literary Fund for supporting my work with a fellowship, and commissioning an early essay on Hilda Boswell's *Treasury of Poetry*. To Tom and Victoria at *The Idler* for asking me to research nonsense, and letting me do my first lecture on 'Fierce Bad Rabbits' in their tent at Port Eliot. To Francesca Dow for meeting with me to talk about the Penguin children's list. To all those who read and commented on earlier drafts, particularly Professor David Rudd, whose advice on the manuscript as both a children's literature expert and family friend from Edgworth was invaluable; my friend Hannah; my husband Richard; my sister Mary, and of course my wonderful mum, who has been my first reader since I was five.

And to Gruff and Cate most of all. Thank you for all the hours spent on my knee letting me read you picture books. They have been some of the best hours of my life.

Index